Real-Time in the Cloud: Azure Messaging & Events

Kameron Hussain and Frahaan Hussain

Published by Kameron Hussain, 2025.

REAL-TIME IN THE CLOUD: AZURE MESSAGING & EVENTS

First edition. May 21, 2025.

ISBN: 979-8231917488

Written by Kameron Hussain and Frahaan Hussain.

Real-Time in the Cloud: Azure Messaging & Events

First Edition

Preface

In today's rapidly evolving digital landscape, the demand for real-time data processing, seamless communication, and responsive systems has become central to user experience and business success. Whether it's processing millions of IoT signals, handling financial transactions in milliseconds, or delivering content updates in near-instant fashion, the need for robust messaging and event-driven architectures is universal.

This book, the *1st Edition* of *Real-Time in the Cloud: Azure Messaging & Events*, is designed to provide a comprehensive, practical, and insightful journey into building modern cloud-based messaging and event-driven systems using Microsoft Azure. It begins by laying a strong conceptual foundation in messaging patterns and architectural styles before exploring the specific services offered by Azure—namely Azure Service Bus, Event Grid, Event Hubs, and Storage Queues.

From understanding the differences between events and messages to implementing high-throughput analytics pipelines and integrating security best practices, this book follows a deliberate progression—from fundamentals to real-world use cases, advanced design considerations, and forward-looking trends in cloud messaging.

Each chapter builds upon the previous ones, equipping readers with both the theoretical knowledge and hands-on strategies needed to architect, implement, monitor, and evolve scalable real-time systems. Real-world case studies are included to ground the theory in practical, industry-specific applications. Whether you're an architect, developer, DevOps engineer, or cloud consultant, this book is your companion for mastering Azure's messaging capabilities.

We've also included appendices to extend learning—offering code snippets, sample projects, and API references to streamline adoption and experimentation.

We hope this book serves not only as a technical guide but as a catalyst for innovation, empowering you to build resilient, responsive, and intelligent cloud-native systems.

Table of Contents

Can I use Logic Apps with Service Bus or Event Grid?

How do I configure private access?

How long are events retained?

Summary

Chapter 1: Introduction

The Evolution of Cloud-Based Real-Time Systems

The landscape of software development and system design has undergone a monumental transformation over the last two decades. The rise of the internet, mobile computing, edge devices, and ubiquitous data generation has redefined what "real-time" means in a production environment. Real-time no longer refers only to milliseconds of response but rather to systems that are always-on, highly available, scalable on demand, and capable of reacting to stimuli instantly—regardless of origin or scale.

From Monoliths to Microservices

In the early days, enterprise applications were monolithic—built as single, massive units. Messaging, if it existed, was internal or batch-based. As demand for scalability and speed increased, microservices emerged, fragmenting applications into independently deployable components. This introduced new communication challenges: How do services talk to each other? How do they stay in sync in a decoupled environment?

Synchronous APIs (like REST) often filled this gap. But they introduced tight coupling, poor fault tolerance, and limited flexibility in high-throughput, burst-prone environments. As a result, asynchronous messaging and event-driven architecture became essential to supporting scalable, loosely coupled microservices and real-time responsiveness.

Real-Time Expectations in a Cloud-Native World

Modern users expect real-time experiences across every domain:

- *Banking:* Immediate transaction alerts
- *Healthcare:* Live telemetry from wearable devices
- *Gaming:* Low-latency multiplayer coordination
- *Retail:* Instant inventory updates
- *Social Media:* Push notifications and live feeds

Meeting these expectations requires systems that ingest, process, and act upon data in real time. This mandates an infrastructure backbone that's not just fast but also elastic, resilient, and geographically distributed. This is where cloud-native paradigms shine, and specifically where Azure's messaging services play a pivotal role.

Event-Driven Design as a First-Class Citizen

Traditional request-response models are linear and fragile under load. Event-driven design, by contrast, treats every state change—user input, file upload, telemetry ping, etc.—as an event to be published and processed asynchronously. This enables:

- **Scalability** by decoupling producers and consumers
- **Resilience** through retry policies, dead-lettering, and buffering
- **Observability** using logs, traces, and metrics around discrete events

- **Flexibility** by supporting multiple independent consumers for a single event

In Azure, services like *Event Grid*, *Event Hubs*, and *Service Bus* make it easy to adopt this paradigm with powerful abstractions and native integrations.

Case Study: Real-Time Logistics Tracking

To illustrate, consider a global logistics company that needs real-time tracking of packages across continents. Each tracking device emits signals every 30 seconds. Instead of direct REST calls into a central system (which would quickly crumble under global scale), devices publish telemetry events to Azure Event Hubs. These are partitioned and consumed in parallel by multiple consumers—some updating dashboards, others feeding AI models, while another enriches metadata in Cosmos DB.

This setup leverages:

- **Azure Event Hubs** for high-throughput ingestion
- **Azure Stream Analytics** for near-real-time processing
- **Azure Functions** for event-based triggers
- **Azure Monitor** for centralized observability

This architecture is elastic, scalable, and resilient, built entirely on Azure-native services.

The Role of Infrastructure-as-Code and DevOps

With the rise of DevOps, infrastructure provisioning and automation have become integral to building real-time systems.

Tools like Azure Resource Manager (ARM) templates, Bicep, and Terraform allow teams to define messaging infrastructure as code—ensuring repeatability and version control.

For example, the following simplified Bicep snippet provisions a namespace and queue in Azure Service Bus:

```
resource sbNamespace 'Microsoft.ServiceBus/namespaces@2022-10-01-preview' = {

name: 'realtime-messaging-ns'

location: 'East US'

sku: {

name: 'Standard'

tier: 'Standard'

}

}

resource sbQueue 'Microsoft.ServiceBus/namespaces/queues@2022-10-01-preview' = {

name: 'event-processing-queue'

parent: sbNamespace

properties: {

maxDeliveryCount: 10

lockDuration: 'PT5M'

requiresDuplicateDetection: true
```

```
}
}
```

This approach supports automated deployments, environment consistency, and integration into CI/CD pipelines, making real-time system development scalable at the team and enterprise level.

Shifting Left on Security and Compliance

Security in real-time systems is not an afterthought. Azure's messaging services provide robust authentication and encryption mechanisms, including:

- **Shared Access Signatures (SAS)**
- **Azure Active Directory (AAD)-based RBAC**
- **Transport Layer Security (TLS)**
- **Message-level encryption and dead-letter auditing**

These capabilities help meet compliance requirements in sensitive industries like finance and healthcare, which mandate data protection in-flight and at rest.

The Data Gravity Problem and Edge Computing

As data volumes grow, transmitting everything to a central cloud for processing becomes impractical due to latency and cost. Edge computing—processing data close to the source—is emerging as a solution. Azure supports this through services like IoT Hub and Azure Stack Edge, where messages can be processed locally and selectively pushed to Event Hubs for aggregation and long-term analytics.

This distributed, hybrid event model is becoming increasingly important in domains such as manufacturing, agriculture, and smart cities.

Summary

The journey toward real-time, event-driven systems is not just a technical shift—it's a change in mindset. Moving from procedural APIs to asynchronous messaging transforms how we build, think about, and operate cloud-native solutions.

Azure provides a rich ecosystem to make this shift seamless, secure, and scalable. From Service Bus to Event Hubs and Event Grid, Microsoft Azure offers the tools to meet the demands of the modern digital enterprise. This chapter laid the groundwork for understanding why real-time systems are more relevant than ever—and why Azure is the right platform to implement them.

In the chapters ahead, we'll delve into the theoretical underpinnings of event-driven architecture, compare Azure's messaging tools, and then go deep into implementation details, monitoring strategies, and future trends. Whether you are modernizing legacy systems or designing greenfield cloud applications, the principles and practices in this book will equip you to succeed in the real-time era.

Why Azure for Messaging and Events?

Modern enterprises increasingly operate in environments where events happen continuously, across disparate systems and geographies. These events could be a temperature reading from a remote IoT sensor, a user clicking "Buy Now" on an e-commerce platform, or a critical transaction processed by a financial system. To capture, route, and react to these events in real time, businesses need a robust and reliable messaging backbone. Microsoft Azure is uniquely positioned to fulfill this need with a suite of mature, scalable, and deeply integrated messaging and event-driven services.

A Unified Platform for Asynchronous Communication

Azure offers multiple specialized services that cater to different patterns of asynchronous communication:

- **Azure Service Bus** for enterprise-grade message brokering with features like dead-letter queues, duplicate detection, transactions, and sessions.

- **Azure Event Grid** for lightweight, low-latency, reactive event publishing and subscription.

- **Azure Event Hubs** for large-scale data ingestion with high throughput and partitioned consumer architectures.

- **Azure Storage Queues** for simple, cost-effective queuing in storage-centric applications.

Together, these services address virtually all modern messaging scenarios—from transactional message processing to massive-scale telemetry pipelines—while maintaining consistent security, observability, and integration with other Azure services.

Deep Integration with the Azure Ecosystem

One of Azure's strongest advantages is its seamless integration across the platform. Messaging services do not exist in isolation; they interact fluidly with:

- **Azure Functions**, enabling event-driven compute with minimal configuration

- **Azure Logic Apps**, offering visual workflows for integration
- **Azure Monitor and Application Insights**, for tracking message throughput, latencies, and failures
- **Azure Active Directory**, enabling role-based access control and secure authentication
- **Azure DevOps and GitHub Actions**, supporting CI/CD pipelines that provision and deploy messaging infrastructure

For instance, consider this simple integration using Azure Functions triggered by a Service Bus queue:

```
[FunctionName("ProcessOrder")]

public async Task Run(

[ServiceBusTrigger("orders", Connection = "ServiceBusConnection")] string orderJson,

ILogger log)

{

var order = JsonConvert.DeserializeObject<Order>(orderJson);

log.LogInformation($"Processing order ID: {order.Id}");

await ProcessOrderAsync(order);

}
```

This function will automatically scale out based on the volume of messages in the orders queue, requiring no manual scaling intervention.

Built for Scale and Global Reach

Azure's messaging services are globally distributed by design. You can deploy resources in multiple regions for high availability, disaster recovery, and low-latency access.

- **Azure Event Hubs** supports throughput units and Auto-Inflate to dynamically scale based on load.
- **Service Bus Premium Tier** provides message processing with guaranteed isolation and higher throughput via dedicated resources.
- **Geo-disaster recovery** and **availability zones** support ensure resilience and continuity for mission-critical workloads.

For global applications—like real-time fraud detection or logistics tracking—this reach and reliability are indispensable.

Rich Feature Set for Real-World Applications

Azure's messaging services come packed with capabilities that address real-world production concerns:

- **Message deduplication** using message ID tracking
- **Scheduled delivery** and **message deferral**
- **Dead-letter queues** for failed or poison messages

- **Sessions** for ordered message processing
- **Transactions** for atomic batch operations
- **Retry and backoff policies** for transient fault handling

Consider a business process where each customer support ticket is processed in order. Service Bus sessions make it possible to ensure in-order delivery for messages belonging to the same session:

```
[FunctionName("ProcessSupportTicket")]

public static void Run(

[ServiceBusTrigger("support-tickets", Connection = "ServiceBusConnection", IsSessionsEnabled = true)]

Message ticketMessage,

ILogger log)

{

var sessionId = ticketMessage.SessionId;

log.LogInformation($"Processing ticket in session: {sessionId}");

}
```

These types of features make Azure services well-suited to building mature, enterprise-ready systems.

Enterprise-Grade Security and Compliance

Azure adheres to some of the most stringent industry certifications and standards, including ISO 27001, SOC 1/2/3, HIPAA, GDPR, and FedRAMP. Messaging services inherit these compliance frameworks, allowing you to build within regulated industries confidently.

Security is enforced through:

- **Transport-level encryption (TLS 1.2 and above)**
- **At-rest encryption with customer-managed keys (CMK) via Azure Key Vault**
- **Role-based access control (RBAC)**
- **Shared Access Signature (SAS) tokens**
- **Private endpoints and virtual network integration**

For highly sensitive applications, you can use the Premium tiers of services to enable full VNet integration and prevent exposure to the public internet entirely.

Serverless-First Architecture Support

Azure Functions, a serverless compute service, natively integrates with Service Bus, Event Grid, and Event Hubs. This allows you to build highly reactive systems with minimal infrastructure overhead. Event-driven, serverless architectures reduce cost, minimize latency, and simplify scaling.

For example, here is a serverless pattern for a telemetry application:

1. Devices send metrics to **Event Hubs**.
2. **Azure Stream Analytics** processes incoming data streams and applies filters.
3. Filtered events are pushed to **Event Grid** for downstream subscribers.

4. **Azure Functions** consume specific events to update dashboards or trigger alerts.

This chain has built-in elasticity, is decoupled, and offers clean separation of concerns.

Developer Productivity and SDK Support

Azure provides mature SDKs in all major programming languages—C#, Java, JavaScript, Python, Go—alongside support for REST APIs. There is strong support in modern development tools like Visual Studio, VS Code, and Azure CLI.

Infrastructure as Code (IaC) tools also streamline developer workflows. Here's a basic Bicep example to create an Event Grid topic:

```
resource topic 'Microsoft.EventGrid/topics@2021-12-01' = {

name: 'sales-events'

location: 'West Europe'

properties: {

inputSchema: 'EventGridSchema'

}

}
```

This allows teams to version, audit, and automate infrastructure, aligning with modern DevOps practices.

Real-World Use Cases on Azure

Azure's messaging services power diverse scenarios across industries:

- **Retail**: Order placement, inventory updates, delivery tracking (Service Bus + Functions)

- **Finance**: Fraud detection and transaction monitoring (Event Hubs + Stream Analytics)

- **Gaming**: Real-time matchmaking and telemetry (Event Hubs + Cosmos DB)

- **Healthcare**: Secure alerts for patient monitoring (Service Bus + Logic Apps)

- **Manufacturing**: IoT-based quality control (IoT Hub + Event Grid)

These use cases often involve large-scale event ingestion, transformation, routing, and action. Azure makes this feasible through its battle-tested infrastructure and first-class support for observability and automation.

Cost Optimization and Tiered Offerings

Azure offers multiple pricing tiers to suit different workloads. You can start small with basic tiers and graduate to Premium or Dedicated clusters as needs grow:

- **Event Grid**: Pay-per-operation pricing, suited for sparse events

- **Service Bus**: Standard and Premium tiers; Premium includes features like message sessions, geo-disaster recovery, and virtual network access

- **Event Hubs**: Standard and Dedicated tiers, with Auto-Inflate and Capture options for optimized analytics pipelines

This tiered model means you can experiment and iterate cost-effectively before scaling up to enterprise capacity.

Observability and Diagnostics

No messaging system is complete without strong observability. Azure provides end-to-end monitoring with:

- **Azure Monitor Metrics**: Message counts, latencies, errors

- **Azure Diagnostic Logs**: Subscription delivery results, dead-letter messages

- **Application Insights**: Custom tracing and performance data

You can set up alerts, dashboards, and automated remediation flows. For example, you can configure an alert when the number of dead-lettered messages in a queue exceeds a threshold, triggering an Azure Function to retry or escalate the issue.

Conclusion

Azure offers a comprehensive, scalable, and secure platform for messaging and events that aligns with modern cloud-native design patterns. Its broad service offerings, developer-friendly tooling, global infrastructure, and deep integration across the Azure ecosystem make it an ideal choice for implementing asynchronous, event-driven architectures.

Whether you are building a global financial application, a healthcare telemetry pipeline, or a real-time gaming backend, Azure provides the building blocks to construct robust, performant, and cost-efficient solutions. In the chapters ahead, we will explore each service in depth, demonstrate design patterns, and walk through practical implementations to help you harness the full power of Azure messaging and event services.

Scope and Structure of This Book

The design, deployment, and management of real-time systems on Azure require a multi-disciplinary understanding of cloud architecture, event-driven patterns, service orchestration, security, and operational excellence. This book is carefully structured to guide readers through all essential aspects—starting from the foundational theory of messaging systems to hands-on implementation and monitoring using Azure's native tools and services. Whether you are an architect designing distributed systems, a developer building event processors, or an operations engineer managing cloud pipelines, this book is crafted to be a practical resource and reference guide.

Audience and Prerequisites

This book is written for a broad audience involved in cloud-native solution development:

- **Software Developers** building applications that need asynchronous processing, reliable messaging, or large-scale event ingestion.

- **Cloud Architects** responsible for designing scalable and fault-tolerant solutions on Microsoft Azure.

- **DevOps Engineers** implementing CI/CD workflows and monitoring pipelines for event-driven services.

- **Data Engineers** working on real-time data collection, processing, and analytics.

- **Solution Consultants** who need to understand trade-offs in selecting the appropriate messaging or event system in Azure.

While we assume familiarity with general cloud computing principles and basic knowledge of Azure services, we introduce every concept from first principles and expand toward complex scenarios. Familiarity with REST APIs, JSON, and at least one programming language (e.g., C#, JavaScript, Python) will help in implementing the code samples, but is not strictly required to understand the concepts.

Book Objectives

By the end of this book, you will be able to:

- Understand the fundamental differences between messages and events and when to use each.

- Design scalable and resilient real-time systems using Azure's native messaging and event services.

- Choose the appropriate Azure service for a given scenario (e.g., Service Bus vs. Event Grid).

- Build pipelines that are secure, observable, and fault-tolerant.

- Operationalize messaging workflows with tools for diagnostics, monitoring, and alerts.

- Analyze real-world implementations to apply lessons learned in production environments.

Chapter Breakdown and Flow

This book is organized into twelve chapters, each focusing on a specific stage of real-time system development and deployment.

Chapter 1: Introduction

We start by exploring the evolution of real-time cloud systems and why Azure is an ideal platform for messaging and event-based solutions. We also provide an overview of the book's structure and key themes.

Chapter 2: Fundamentals of Messaging and Event-Driven Architecture

This chapter introduces the conceptual foundations, contrasting messaging and events, and detailing the characteristics of event-driven architectures (EDA). We explore benefits like decoupling, flexibility, and fault tolerance, while also addressing challenges such as message ordering, duplication, and schema evolution.

Chapter 3: Overview of Azure Messaging Services

We cover the major Azure services designed for messaging and event-driven patterns:

- Azure Service Bus
- Azure Event Grid
- Azure Event Hubs

- Azure Storage Queues

Each service is introduced with use cases, technical features, performance characteristics, and pricing considerations. We close with a comparative matrix to assist in service selection.

Chapter 4: Designing Real-Time Solutions with Azure

This chapter takes a design-first approach. We explore architectural patterns such as event sourcing, CQRS (Command Query Responsibility Segregation), pub-sub models, fan-out patterns, and stateful message processing. Special attention is given to scalability techniques (partitioning, load balancing) and security strategies (RBAC, private endpoints).

Chapter 5: Implementing Azure Service Bus

In this hands-on chapter, you'll learn how to set up namespaces, queues, and topics. We'll demonstrate message creation, serialization, and processing using SDKs in .NET and JavaScript. Topics include dead-letter queues, message sessions, and integration with Azure Functions and Logic Apps.

```
// Sample: Sending a message to a queue

var client = new ServiceBusClient(connectionString);

var sender = client.CreateSender("order-queue");

await sender.SendMessageAsync(new ServiceBusMessage("Order received"));
```

Chapter 6: Mastering Azure Event Grid

You'll dive into custom events, domains, advanced routing, and filtering strategies. Event Grid's role in reactive architecture, webhook patterns, and third-party integrations will also be covered. Security via SAS tokens, Event Subscriptions, and Managed Identity will be demonstrated.

Chapter 7: Harnessing Azure Event Hubs

This chapter focuses on high-throughput, distributed event ingestion. You'll learn about partitions, consumer groups, and offset tracking. Integration with Azure Stream Analytics and Apache Kafka will be explored in detail.

Chapter 8: Real-World Use Cases and Case Studies

We present practical, domain-specific applications:

- IoT systems for telemetry collection
- Fintech systems for real-time fraud detection
- Healthcare systems for patient event notifications
- Media pipelines for ingesting video metadata

These examples include architecture diagrams, service selections, data flows, and implementation tips based on real Azure projects.

Chapter 9: Monitoring, Troubleshooting, and Maintaining Azure Messaging Systems

Every production system needs robust monitoring. This chapter covers setting up logs, alerts, dashboards, and automated recovery workflows using Azure Monitor, Log Analytics, and custom telemetry. Topics like failure patterns, retries, circuit breakers, and cold start mitigation are addressed.

Chapter 10: Future Trends in Cloud Messaging and Events

We explore what's coming next—event mesh patterns, distributed tracing, 5G and edge integration, AI-enhanced event processing, and open standards like CloudEvents. You'll understand how Azure is evolving to support these trends.

Chapter 11: Conclusion

A summary of lessons learned, final recommendations, and suggestions for continued study. We'll also highlight key takeaways for different roles—developers, architects, and operations teams.

Chapter 12: Appendices

Includes a glossary of key terms, API reference snippets, and additional resources (Microsoft Learn, GitHub samples, open-source tools). Sample projects will provide a practical starting point for building end-to-end solutions.

How to Use This Book

You can read the book linearly or use it as a reference guide:

- If you're **new to messaging**, read Chapters 1–4 in sequence.
- If you want to **implement a solution**, jump to Chapters 5–7 for hands-on instructions.
- If you're evaluating **service suitability**, see Chapter 3's comparison section.
- For **ongoing operations**, Chapter 9 provides best practices.

- For **strategic planning**, Chapter 10 will inform roadmap considerations.

Tools and Environment Used

Throughout this book, we will use:

- **Azure Portal** for initial exploration
- **Azure CLI** and **Azure PowerShell** for scripting
- **Bicep/Terraform** for Infrastructure-as-Code
- **Visual Studio Code** and **Visual Studio 2022**
- SDKs in **C#**, **Python**, and **JavaScript**

Code examples are simplified for clarity but represent best practices and real-world patterns. All code and templates will be made available via a public GitHub repository linked in the appendix.

Conventions

- **Azure CLI** commands are prefixed with az.
- Code is formatted in code blocks per language (C#, Python, JavaScript).
- Key terms are *italicized* and concepts are **bolded** for emphasis.
- Diagrams and visuals are described where relevant but not shown in this text-based format.

Summary

This book's structure mirrors the lifecycle of a real-time messaging solution—from inception to design, deployment, operation, and future evolution. By the end, you will not only understand Azure's messaging landscape but also be capable of architecting systems that are resilient, scalable, and event-driven.

We now invite you to dive deeper into the theory and practice of cloud messaging, beginning with a foundational look at how messages and events differ, how they enable powerful patterns, and how they shape the future of cloud-native applications.

Chapter 2: Fundamentals of Messaging and Event-Driven Architecture

Understanding Messaging vs. Events

In the realm of distributed computing and real-time cloud systems, the terms "messaging" and "events" are often used interchangeably. However, they represent fundamentally different communication models, semantics, and system behaviors. Understanding the distinctions between them is critical to choosing the right Azure services, applying the correct architectural patterns, and achieving desired outcomes in scalability, performance, and maintainability.

Messaging: Commands, Contracts, and Control

Messaging is a pattern of communication where one component sends a *message* to another to perform a specific action. The message is typically structured, often governed by a defined schema, and contains explicit instructions or data required for the receiving system to act upon.

Key characteristics of messaging include:

- **Intent:** Messages are often commands ("create an order", "process a payment") that expect some form of action.

- **Point-to-point or publish-subscribe delivery:** Messaging can be unicast (one sender to one receiver) or multicast (one to many).

- **Strong coupling to schema:** Receivers usually require well-defined message structures to process them correctly.

- **Guaranteed delivery:** Systems like Azure Service Bus offer transactional integrity, retries, and dead-lettering to ensure that messages are delivered reliably.

- **Stateful workflows:** Messaging is often used in orchestrating complex, multi-step workflows, such as order fulfillment or claims processing.

In this paradigm, communication resembles a contract—"I (the sender) expect you (the receiver) to do something specific, and I've given you everything you need to do it."

Example Use Case:

A warehouse management system sends a message to a shipping service:

{ "orderId": "A12345", "action": "ship", "priority": "express" }

This message may be pushed to a queue where a worker listens for incoming shipping requests and processes them in order.

```
public class ShippingWorker

{

public async Task ProcessMessageAsync(string message)

{

var request = JsonSerializer.Deserialize<ShippingRequest>(message);

await ShipOrderAsync(request.OrderId);

}
```

}

Events: Facts, Observations, and Loose Coupling

Events are records of something that *has already happened* in the system. They are declarative and broadcast in nature. Rather than instructing a system to do something, an event says, "This happened"—and it is up to subscribers to decide how to react.

Key characteristics of events include:

- **Past tense:** Events are emitted after an action or state change occurs. For example, "OrderCreated", "UserSignedIn", or "PaymentFailed".

- **Decoupling:** Event producers do not know or care about their consumers. This allows for high flexibility and system evolution over time.

- **One-to-many delivery:** Events can be published once and consumed by many independent services.

- **Immutability:** Events should not be changed or deleted once published. This makes them suitable for audit trails and event sourcing.

- **Idempotency:** Since multiple consumers may receive the same event, handlers must be designed to be idempotent—processing the event repeatedly should not change the result.

Example Use Case:

An e-commerce platform emits an OrderCreated event. Multiple systems might subscribe to it:

- A **billing system** to initiate payment.
- A **logistics service** to reserve inventory.
- A **notification engine** to email the customer.

Each of these is independent and unaware of the others. This is a key feature of event-driven design.

```
{
"eventType": "OrderCreated",
"subject": "order/A12345",
"data": {
"orderId": "A12345",
"customerId": "C67890",
"timestamp": "2025-05-09T10:00:00Z"
}
}
```

Messaging vs. Events: A Comparative Table

Feature	Messaging	Events
Purpose	Command, request	Notification, signal
Producer expectation	Action to be taken	No response expected
Coupling	Tightly coupled schema	Loosely coupled consumers
Delivery pattern	Point-to-point or pub-sub	Typically pub-sub
Processing sequence	Often ordered	Typically unordered
Typical Azure Service	Azure Service Bus, Storage Queues	Azure Event Grid, Azure Event Hubs
Fault handling	Retries, dead-letter queues	Drop or log errors
Use in workflows	Orchestration	Choreography

When to Use Messaging

Messaging is best suited for use cases where:

- Actions must be taken in a particular sequence.
- Reliable delivery is critical.
- Schema validation and message contracts are strictly enforced.
- Systems must coordinate in a tightly controlled workflow.

Examples:

- Order processing pipelines
- Payment gateways
- Document approval workflows

```
await serviceBusSender.SendMessageAsync(
new ServiceBusMessage(JsonSerializer.Serialize(orderRequest))
{
MessageId = orderRequest.OrderId,
ScheduledEnqueueTime =
DateTimeOffset.UtcNow.AddSeconds(5)
});
```

When to Use Events

Events are best when:

- Systems need to scale independently.
- New consumers may be added dynamically.
- You're building a reactive system or implementing event sourcing.
- You want to capture system activity for analytics or machine learning.

Examples:

- Application telemetry and usage statistics

- Inventory restocking notifications
- Customer behavior tracking (e.g., "ItemViewed")

```
def publish_order_event(order_id):
event = {
"eventType": "OrderCreated",
"subject": f"order/{order_id}",
"data": {"orderId": order_id},
"eventTime": datetime.utcnow().isoformat()
}
event_grid_client.send(event)
```

Hybrid Patterns

Many real-world systems combine messaging and events.

Scenario: A payment system receives a message instructing it to charge a customer. Once the charge is complete, it emits an event PaymentSucceeded.

- The message initiates the workflow (imperative).
- The event signals completion (declarative).

This separation ensures clear system boundaries, fault isolation, and observability.

Role of Azure Services

Azure provides first-class support for both models:

- **Azure Service Bus**: Robust messaging for high-reliability workflows.
- **Azure Event Grid**: Lightweight event distribution to many handlers.
- **Azure Event Hubs**: High-volume event ingestion for analytics and stream processing.
- **Azure Storage Queues**: Basic queueing for lightweight or cost-sensitive apps.

Choosing the right tool requires understanding the communication pattern. The next chapters will guide you in that selection process.

Summary

The distinction between messaging and events is not academic—it has deep architectural consequences. Messaging focuses on command-based communication with control over delivery, sequence, and transactional integrity. Events, by contrast, promote loosely coupled, scalable, and reactive systems that evolve independently and scale elastically.

Understanding when to use each model—and often combining both—is a hallmark of mature cloud-native design. As you progress through this book, you will learn how to select, design, implement, and scale these patterns effectively using Microsoft Azure.

Core Concepts of Event-Driven Systems

Event-driven systems are a cornerstone of modern, cloud-native application design. These systems are characterized by their reactive, decoupled, and asynchronous nature, enabling applications to respond to changes in state or external stimuli in real-time. At their heart, event-driven systems are built upon the idea of *events* as first-class entities—signals that indicate something has happened and may require downstream action. This section explores the core concepts that define event-driven architecture (EDA), including event producers and consumers, event brokers, event schemas, choreography versus orchestration, and the importance of idempotency, observability, and scalability.

Event Producers and Event Consumers

At the most fundamental level, an event-driven system comprises two primary roles: **event producers** and **event consumers**.

- **Event Producers** are components or services that detect a change in state and emit an event. Examples include a user submitting a form, an IoT sensor reporting data, or a service completing a transaction.

- **Event Consumers** are components or services that subscribe to, receive, and process events. A single event can be consumed by multiple consumers, each performing independent operations.

These roles are logically and physically decoupled. A producer emits an event without knowing who will consume it, when it will be processed, or how it will be handled. This loose coupling enhances scalability, resilience, and maintainability.

{

"eventType": "OrderShipped",

"subject": "orders/ORD-1001",

"data": {

"orderId": "ORD-1001",

"shipmentId": "SHIP-5678",

"shippedAt": "2025-05-09T14:32:00Z"

}

}

In this example, the OrderShipped event could be consumed by:

- A customer notification service
- An inventory update service
- A delivery tracking system

None of these need to know about the others.

Event Brokers and Topics

In real-world architectures, direct communication between producers and consumers is uncommon. Instead, events are routed through **event brokers**, which act as intermediaries. These brokers decouple producers from consumers and offer features like filtering, retries, durability, and access control.

Azure provides several broker options:

- **Azure Event Grid**: Ideal for lightweight, reactive routing with support for filters and retries.
- **Azure Event Hubs**: Optimized for high-throughput, time-ordered ingestion of telemetry and logs.

- **Azure Service Bus Topics**: Support advanced message routing and subscription models, including sessions and filters.

An event broker typically supports **topics** or **streams**, where events are published and then subscribed to by one or more consumers.

```
resource eventHubNamespace 'Microsoft.EventHub/namespaces@2022-10-01-preview' = {

name: 'analytics-hub'

location: 'East US'

sku: {

name: 'Standard'

tier: 'Standard'

}

}

resource eventHub 'Microsoft.EventHub/namespaces/eventhubs@2022-10-01-preview' = {

name: 'user-click-events'

parent: eventHubNamespace

}
```

This Bicep code sets up an Event Hub for telemetry ingestion in Azure, which can then be consumed by multiple downstream processors such as Azure Stream Analytics or Azure Functions.

Event Schema and Contracts

Events are data structures. A well-defined **event schema** is critical for interoperability between producers and consumers. A typical event schema includes:

- eventType: A string that identifies what happened.
- subject: The logical resource associated with the event.
- eventTime: When the event occurred.
- data: A payload with relevant context and details.
- id: A unique identifier for deduplication and tracing.
- dataVersion: To support evolution of the schema over time.

Azure Event Grid supports the **CloudEvents** standard, a CNCF-backed specification designed to promote event interoperability across platforms.

```
{
"specversion": "1.0",
"type": "com.warehouse.inventory.lowstock",
"source": "/inventory/warehouse1",
"id": "abc-123-xyz",
"time": "2025-05-09T12:00:00Z",
"datacontenttype": "application/json",
```

"data": {

"itemId": "SKU-5678",

"available": 4,

"threshold": 5

}

}

Using consistent schemas enables validation, routing, and integration with third-party systems.

Choreography vs. Orchestration

In distributed systems, **orchestration** and **choreography** refer to how components coordinate their behavior.

- **Orchestration** involves a central controller that dictates the sequence of tasks across services. Each service acts on explicit instructions from the orchestrator.

- **Choreography** is a decentralized model where services react to events and determine their own behavior. There is no central authority; coordination emerges from the flow of events.

Event-driven systems favor choreography. For example:

1. An order is placed → emits OrderCreated
2. Inventory service consumes OrderCreated → checks stock → emits InventoryReserved
3. Billing service consumes InventoryReserved → charges the user → emits PaymentCompleted

4. Shipping service consumes PaymentCompleted → dispatches item

Each step is autonomous, resilient to failure, and independently scalable.

Idempotency and Deduplication

In an event-driven system, events may be delivered more than once due to retries or system faults. **Idempotency** ensures that processing the same event multiple times yields the same result. This is essential for maintaining data integrity and avoiding side effects like double billing or duplicate emails.

Strategies for idempotency:

- Use **event IDs** to track processed events in a cache or database.
- Implement **natural idempotency**, such as UPSERT operations in SQL.
- Ensure side-effecting operations (e.g., sending SMS) are guarded against duplication.

```
MERGE INTO Orders AS Target

USING (SELECT @OrderId AS OrderId, @Status AS Status) AS Source

ON Target.OrderId = Source.OrderId

WHEN MATCHED THEN UPDATE SET Target.Status = Source.Status
```

```
WHEN NOT MATCHED THEN INSERT (OrderId, Status)
VALUES (Source.OrderId, Source.Status);
```

This SQL operation avoids duplicate inserts and can be used safely in event processing.

Observability and Monitoring

In complex event-driven systems, observability is essential. Since events propagate asynchronously, tracing execution flow is non-trivial. Azure offers several tools:

- **Application Insights** for distributed tracing.
- **Azure Monitor Logs** for aggregating logs from Functions, Event Hubs, and Logic Apps.
- **Azure Metrics Explorer** to visualize throughput, latency, and error rates.
- **Activity IDs and Correlation IDs** to trace a request across multiple services.

Designing systems with correlation in mind from the beginning makes debugging and performance tuning vastly more manageable.

```
var telemetry = new TelemetryClient();

telemetry.Context.Operation.Id = correlationId;

telemetry.TrackEvent("InventoryReserved", new Dictionary<string, string>

{

{ "orderId", orderId },
```

```
{ "warehouse", "WHS-1" }
});
```

Event Versioning and Evolution

As systems evolve, so too do the schemas of emitted events. This must be managed carefully to avoid breaking consumers.

Best practices include:

- **Include a dataVersion** field.
- **Avoid removing fields**; mark them as deprecated.
- **Add new fields as optional**, not required.
- **Use schema registries or API contracts** for validation.

Consumers should be tolerant of unknown fields and able to process multiple versions of an event.

Replay and Event Persistence

In many scenarios, especially in analytics and auditing, it is valuable to **replay** past events. This is only possible if the event broker supports persistence.

- **Azure Event Hubs** supports a configurable retention window and offset tracking.
- **Event Sourcing** patterns store events as the primary record of state.

In these cases, the event log becomes the source of truth, and applications reconstruct state by replaying the event stream.

Event-Driven Transaction Patterns

Distributed systems often need to maintain consistency across services. This is challenging in an asynchronous, eventually consistent model. Popular patterns include:

- **Outbox Pattern:** Events are written to a database table in the same transaction as business data and later published by a background process.
- **SAGA Pattern:** A series of local transactions coordinated via events, with compensating actions for rollback.
- **Transactional Messaging:** Using tools like Azure Service Bus that support atomic send-and-store operations.

These patterns allow building reliable systems that maintain business consistency without distributed transactions.

Summary

Event-driven systems enable loosely coupled, highly scalable, and reactive architectures that are foundational to cloud-native development. By understanding the roles of producers, consumers, brokers, and schemas—and by designing for idempotency, observability, and versioning—you can construct systems that are resilient, extensible, and ready for real-time demands.

In the following sections, we will explore the tangible benefits and challenges of this model, and show how Azure's services allow you to implement these principles effectively at scale.

Benefits and Challenges in Real-Time Cloud Communications

The evolution of cloud platforms has enabled organizations to build systems that are not only globally distributed and scalable but also capable of responding to events as they happen. Real-time cloud communication is no longer a luxury or niche requirement—it is a fundamental expectation in modern applications. Whether it's a ride-sharing platform tracking drivers in real-time, a financial trading platform reacting to market changes within milliseconds, or a healthcare application delivering critical alerts, the importance of low-latency, responsive systems cannot be overstated.

This section explores the **key benefits** and **common challenges** of building real-time systems in the cloud, with a particular emphasis on messaging and event-driven models. It also addresses how Azure services and design principles can help mitigate these challenges while amplifying the advantages.

Benefits of Real-Time Cloud Communication

1. Improved User Experience

Real-time responsiveness enhances the user experience by providing immediate feedback and interaction. For instance:

- Chat applications deliver messages instantly.
- Live dashboards update with the latest sensor or financial data.
- Ecommerce sites reflect current stock levels and pricing dynamically.

This immediacy makes applications feel intelligent, interactive, and reliable.

```
// SignalR example for real-time notifications
const connection = new signalR.HubConnectionBuilder()
.withUrl("/notificationsHub")
.build();
connection.on("ReceiveNotification", (message) => {
showToast(message);
});
```

Azure SignalR Service helps deliver real-time push notifications to web and mobile clients with minimal latency.

2. System Decoupling and Maintainability

Event-driven architectures promote loose coupling between components. This results in systems that are easier to maintain, extend, and scale independently.

For example, when an OrderPlaced event is emitted:

- One microservice can handle invoicing.
- Another updates inventory.
- A third sends customer notifications.

These services operate independently, without the emitter needing to know who consumes the events.

3. Scalability and Elasticity

Real-time systems in the cloud can scale dynamically based on workload:

- **Azure Event Hubs** supports Auto-Inflate for throughput units.
- **Azure Functions** scales instances based on event volume.
- **Service Bus Queues** buffer workloads to allow asynchronous processing at sustainable rates.

This elasticity prevents bottlenecks and ensures cost-efficient operations by allocating resources on demand.

4. Resilience and Fault Isolation

Event-driven systems are inherently resilient:

- Failures in one consumer do not affect others.
- Retry and dead-letter mechanisms prevent message loss.
- Queues and topics act as shock absorbers between services.

This design promotes fault isolation and graceful degradation during incidents.

5. Real-Time Analytics and Insights

Real-time communication facilitates instant data analysis. With tools like **Azure Stream Analytics**, you can:

- Monitor temperature trends across IoT devices.
- Detect anomalies in financial transactions.
- Analyze customer behavior on an ecommerce platform.

These insights drive faster decision-making and more adaptive systems.

```
SELECT

deviceId,

AVG(temperature) AS avgTemp

INTO

output

FROM

input TIMESTAMP BY time

GROUP BY

deviceId, TumblingWindow(minute, 5)
```

This query computes rolling 5-minute averages from a real-time stream.

6. Enhanced Operational Agility

Event-driven models enable organizations to quickly integrate new services without disrupting existing ones. Adding a new consumer to a topic or event stream does not require changes to the producer, allowing for rapid innovation and experimentation.

This supports A/B testing, progressive rollouts, and rapid iteration—hallmarks of modern DevOps culture.

Challenges in Real-Time Cloud Communication

Despite the benefits, building and operating real-time systems in the cloud introduces several challenges. These must be addressed through robust architecture, tooling, and operational strategies.

1. Complexity of Asynchronous Systems

Asynchronous, distributed systems are inherently more complex than synchronous ones. Challenges include:

- Understanding event flow across services.
- Debugging when something goes wrong (e.g., a message is processed twice or out of order).
- Ensuring eventual consistency.

Effective logging, correlation IDs, and tracing frameworks are essential to manage this complexity.

```
logger.LogInformation("OrderProcessed", new { CorrelationId = correlationId, OrderId = orderId });
```

Azure Application Insights can aggregate and visualize logs across services for end-to-end traceability.

2. Event Ordering and Delivery Guarantees

Not all Azure services guarantee ordered delivery or exactly-once processing. For example:

- **Event Hubs** offers at-least-once delivery with partitioning, not global ordering.
- **Event Grid** delivers events at least once but does not preserve order.

Developers must:

- Design idempotent handlers.
- Handle out-of-order events.
- Implement de-duplication where necessary.

3. State Management

In real-time systems, state is often distributed and transient. Managing state reliably requires:

- Persisting key information in durable storage (e.g., Cosmos DB, Azure SQL).
- Using **event sourcing** where the event log is the primary source of truth.

- Handling eventual consistency in a way that meets business expectations.


```
{
"eventType": "InventoryAdjusted",
"data": {
"productId": "SKU-00123",
"change": -4,
"newQuantity": 96
}
}
```


If this event is delayed, systems depending on accurate stock levels may behave inconsistently unless compensated.

4. Security and Access Control

Real-time systems often expose APIs or data streams. Security considerations include:

- Protecting message integrity and confidentiality.
- Validating event sources and payloads.
- Managing access through Azure RBAC, SAS tokens, or Managed Identities.

For instance, with **Azure Event Grid**, you can:

- Use **event subscription filters** to limit exposure.

- Apply **dead-lettering** for unprocessable events.
- Monitor event delivery with **metrics and diagnostics logs.**

5. Operational Overhead and Monitoring

Running a real-time system in production means being proactive:

- Are events being dropped or delayed?
- Are consumers falling behind?
- Are retries flooding downstream services?

Azure tools like **Monitor**, **Log Analytics**, and **Service Health** help address these questions, but they must be correctly configured from day one.

6. Cost Management

Real-time communication can be expensive at scale. Considerations include:

- Cost per million operations in Event Grid.
- Throughput units in Event Hubs.
- Function executions triggered by events.
- Retention, diagnostics, and ingestion in monitoring services.

Best practices:

- Use batching where supported.
- Expire stale messages.
- Archive old events to cold storage for compliance without high operational costs.

Design Best Practices for Mitigating Challenges

To realize the full benefits of real-time systems while minimizing risks:

- **Design for failure:** Assume services will fail, and build with retries, dead-letter queues, and fallback logic.
- **Keep consumers idempotent:** Always ensure safe re-processing of events.
- **Instrument everything:** Use logs, metrics, and tracing to observe the system in real time.
- **Start simple:** Don't over-engineer. Start with basic patterns and evolve with usage.
- **Use the right Azure service:** Understand the trade-offs between Event Grid, Event Hubs, Service Bus, and Storage Queues.

Summary

Real-time cloud communication unlocks powerful new capabilities—from dynamic user experiences to operational agility and data-driven automation. However, the asynchronous, distributed nature of these systems brings architectural and operational complexity that must be addressed intentionally.

By leveraging the strengths of Azure's native messaging and event services, adopting proven patterns, and building with observability, security, and scalability in mind, organizations can create real-time systems that are not only performant but also resilient, maintainable, and future-proof.

In the next chapter, we'll explore Azure's messaging services in detail, comparing their capabilities and understanding how to choose the right one for each use case.

Chapter 3: Overview of Azure Messaging Services

Azure Service Bus

Azure Service Bus is Microsoft's enterprise-grade messaging platform designed for decoupled communication between components and applications, particularly in complex systems that require reliable message delivery, transactions, and sophisticated routing patterns. As a fully managed Platform-as-a-Service (PaaS), it allows applications to interact through durable message queues and publish/subscribe topics without direct dependency on each other's availability or implementation.

Service Bus supports both **message queuing** and **topic-based publish/subscribe** communication, making it versatile for a wide variety of integration scenarios in enterprise and cloud-native architectures.

Key Features and Capabilities

1. Message Queues

At its core, Service Bus provides FIFO (First In, First Out) message queues. A queue stores messages until they are consumed by a single consumer. This is ideal for load leveling, buffering workloads, and maintaining asynchronous communication between services.

- **Max message size**: Up to 256 KB (Standard), 1 MB (Premium)
- **Message TTL**: Configurable per message or queue

- **Peek-lock** mode to safely process messages without losing them on failure

```
resource serviceBusNamespace 'Microsoft.ServiceBus/namespaces@2022-10-01-preview' = {
name: 'enterprise-bus'
location: 'West Europe'
sku: {
name: 'Premium'
tier: 'Premium'
}
}
resource orderQueue 'Microsoft.ServiceBus/namespaces/queues@2022-10-01-preview' = {
name: 'order-queue'
parent: serviceBusNamespace
properties: {
maxDeliveryCount: 10
requiresDuplicateDetection: true
duplicateDetectionHistoryTimeWindow: 'PT10M'
lockDuration: 'PT5M'
}
```

```
}
```

This Bicep snippet provisions a durable queue with deduplication and a 5-minute lock timeout, commonly used in transactional systems.

2. Topics and Subscriptions

In more complex scenarios, **topics and subscriptions** enable publish/subscribe messaging. A topic allows multiple independent subscribers to receive a copy of each message. This model supports sophisticated fan-out scenarios and message routing based on filters and rules.

- Each **subscription** acts like a virtual queue.
- **SQL-like filters** define which messages are delivered to each subscription.
- Subscriptions can have auto-forwarding, dead-lettering, and message TTL.

```
// Creating a subscription with a filter
await adminClient.CreateSubscriptionAsync(
new CreateSubscriptionOptions("orders-topic", "high-priority"),
new CreateRuleOptions("priority-filter", new SqlRuleFilter("priority = 'high'")));
```

This setup ensures only high-priority messages reach the high-priority subscription.

3. Sessions

Service Bus supports **sessions** for grouping related messages that must be processed in order. This is useful for workflows that involve a sequence of events per entity (e.g., per customer, per order).

- Enables FIFO message processing per session.
- Supports automatic session locking and safe concurrent processing.

```
[FunctionName("ProcessOrderSession")]

public static async Task Run(

[ServiceBusTrigger("order-queue", IsSessionsEnabled = true)] ServiceBusReceivedMessage message,

ServiceBusSessionReceiver receiver,

ILogger log)

{

var orderId = message.SessionId;

log.LogInformation($"Processing order session: {orderId}");

}
```

This Azure Function ensures ordered processing for all messages associated with a specific session ID.

4. Transactions

Azure Service Bus allows multiple operations—send, receive, complete—to be grouped into an atomic transaction. This guarantees that either all operations succeed or none do.

Use cases include:

- Receiving a message, updating a database, and sending a new message.
- Chaining multiple queue operations within a workflow.

5. Dead-Letter Queues (DLQs)

DLQs are built-in sub-queues used for messages that cannot be processed, such as:

- Reaching maximum delivery attempts
- Failing to match subscription filters
- Explicit dead-lettering by a consumer

Messages in DLQs can be inspected, reprocessed, or moved to alternate queues, supporting operational diagnostics and recovery.

6. Scheduled Messages and Deferred Delivery

Service Bus supports **delayed delivery** of messages, allowing tasks to be postponed without requiring timers or cron jobs.

```
var message = new ServiceBusMessage("send later")
{
```

```
ScheduledEnqueueTime = DateTimeOffset.UtcNow.AddMinutes(10)

};

await sender.SendMessageAsync(message);
```

This is useful for workflows like retry after delay, scheduled notifications, or timed business rules.

7. Integration and Triggers

Service Bus is deeply integrated with other Azure services:

- **Azure Functions**: Event-driven serverless processing
- **Logic Apps**: Low-code workflow automation
- **Azure API Management**: Securing queue access via REST
- **Azure Key Vault**: Securing connection strings and secrets

You can use bindings in Azure Functions to easily create event-driven workflows:

```
[FunctionName("QueueTriggerFunction")]

public async Task Run(

[ServiceBusTrigger("email-queue", Connection = "ServiceBusConnection")] string message,

ILogger log)
```

```
{
log.LogInformation($"Email job: {message}");
}
```

8. Advanced Features (Premium Tier)

The **Premium tier** unlocks additional features including:

- **Virtual Network (VNet) Integration**
- **Private endpoints**
- **Zone redundancy**
- **Higher throughput and scalability**
- **Dedicated resources for consistent performance**

This makes the Premium tier ideal for regulated industries, low-latency SLAs, and mission-critical systems.

Typical Use Cases

- **Order Processing Pipelines**: Queue-based message handling with retries and tracking.
- **Approval Workflows**: Session-based orchestration of human-in-the-loop approvals.
- **Financial Transactions**: Guaranteed delivery and sequencing of operations.

- **Email and Notification Systems**: Decoupled task processing and delayed messages.
- **Microservice Communication**: Topic-based messaging for multiple service subscribers.

Service Bus vs Other Azure Messaging Services

Feature	Azure Service Bus	Azure Event Grid	Azure Event Hubs
Delivery Guarantee	At-least-once	At-least-once	At-least-once
Message Size Limit	256 KB / 1 MB	1 MB	1 MB
FIFO Ordering	Supported (via sessions)	Not guaranteed	Supported (per partition)
Dead-Lettering	Yes	No	No
Message TTL	Yes	Yes	Yes
Push vs Pull	Pull	Push	Pull
Target Use Case	Enterprise workflows	Reactive events	Telemetry ingestion

Monitoring and Diagnostics

Azure provides several mechanisms to monitor and manage Service Bus:

- **Azure Monitor**: Built-in metrics like ActiveMessages, DeadLetteredMessages, IncomingRequests, ThrottledRequests.

- **Diagnostic Settings**: Forward logs to Log Analytics, Event Hubs, or Storage.
- **Application Insights**: End-to-end tracing with correlation IDs.

Example: Creating an alert when DLQ grows:

```
resource alert 'Microsoft.Insights/metricAlerts@2018-03-01' = {
name: 'DeadLetterQueueAlert'
location: 'global'
properties: {
severity: 2
enabled: true
scopes: [orderQueue.id]
evaluationFrequency: 'PT1M'
windowSize: 'PT5M'
criteria: {
allOf: [
{
metricName: 'DeadLetteredMessages'
timeAggregation: 'Total'
operator: 'GreaterThan'
threshold: 10
```

```
}
]
}
actions: []
}
}
```

Cost Considerations

Azure Service Bus pricing is based on tier, number of operations, and features used. Key pricing metrics include:

- Number of messages sent/received
- Delivery attempts (including retries)
- Premium units for throughput and isolation

Optimization tips:

- Use batching to reduce operations.
- Expire unused messages.
- Monitor usage and scale queues/topics accordingly.

Summary

Azure Service Bus is a powerful and reliable messaging backbone that supports enterprise-grade messaging scenarios with features like transactions, dead-letter queues, message sessions, and advanced routing. It is ideal for mission-critical applications that require guaranteed delivery, decoupled workflows, and secure, ordered communication between distributed systems.

In the next sections, we will explore Event Grid and Event Hubs—two complementary services designed for event distribution and high-throughput data ingestion respectively—helping you understand where each service fits best in the Azure messaging landscape.

Azure Event Grid

Azure Event Grid is a fully managed event routing service that enables the development of reactive, event-driven applications in the cloud. Unlike traditional message queues, Event Grid is optimized for lightweight, high-scale event distribution across services and regions. It allows applications and services to publish events to a central event broker and enables subscribers to act upon those events without direct coupling to the publishers.

Event Grid provides a publish-subscribe model, where producers (event sources) emit events, and consumers (event handlers) subscribe to them via event subscriptions. It excels at broadcasting discrete facts about changes in state, supporting rich integrations with Azure services, custom topics, and third-party endpoints via webhooks.

Core Concepts

Event Sources

Event sources are services or applications that generate events. Event Grid supports a broad range of native sources including:

- Azure Blob Storage (e.g., blob created/deleted)

- Azure Resource Groups (e.g., resource created/ updated)
- Azure Event Hubs, IoT Hub, Media Services
- Custom applications publishing to **custom topics**


```
{
"eventType": "Contoso.Items.ItemCreated",
"subject": "/items/item123",
"data": {
"itemId": "item123",
"createdBy": "user456",
"timestamp": "2025-05-09T12:00:00Z"
},
"eventTime": "2025-05-09T12:00:00Z",
"id": "a1b2c3d4",
"dataVersion": "1.0"
}
```


This event schema conforms to Event Grid's native format and is based on the CloudEvents specification.

Topics

A **topic** is the entry point to Event Grid. It represents a category of events that consumers can subscribe to. Azure provides:

- **System topics**: Automatically created for Azure resources (e.g., Blob Storage).
- **Custom topics**: User-defined topics that custom apps and external services can publish to.

Example Bicep for a custom topic:

```
resource eventGridTopic 'Microsoft.EventGrid/topics@2021-12-01' = {

name: 'order-events'

location: 'East US'

properties: {

inputSchema: 'EventGridSchema'

}

}
```

You can now publish to order-events using an authenticated HTTPS POST.

Event Subscriptions

Consumers subscribe to a topic via an **event subscription**. Each subscription defines:

- A **destination** (e.g., Azure Function, Logic App, Event Hub, webhook)
- Optional **filters** on event type or subject pattern
- **Retry policies**, **dead-lettering**, and **event TTLs**

Example filter: Only forward OrderShipped events to a specific Function.

```
resource orderShippedSubscription 'Microsoft.EventGrid/topics/eventSubscriptions@2021-12-01' = {
name: 'order-shipped-sub'
parent: eventGridTopic
properties: {
destination: {
endpointType: 'AzureFunction'
properties: {
resourceId: '/subscriptions/.../functions/OrderShippedHandler'
}
}
filter: {
includedEventTypes: ['OrderShipped']
}
}
```

}

This flexibility allows precise control over how and where events are routed.

Delivery Semantics and Reliability

Event Grid guarantees **at-least-once delivery**, with built-in retry logic:

- Exponential backoff with up to 24-hour retry window
- 30-second default timeout for event handler response
- Dead-lettering to Storage Blob in case of repeated failures

To ensure **resilience**, consumers should be:

- Idempotent
- Capable of handling out-of-order delivery
- Designed to detect and ignore duplicate events

Dead-Lettering

For durable error handling, Event Grid can forward undeliverable events to a **dead-letter blob container**. These events can be reprocessed manually or via automated workflows.

properties: {

deadLetterDestination: {

endpointType: 'StorageBlob'

```
properties: {
resourceId: '/subscriptions/.../storageAccounts/myStorage'
blobContainerName: 'deadletters'
}
}
}
```

This supports robust diagnostics and operational integrity.

Native Integrations

One of Event Grid's core strengths is its deep integration with Azure and third-party platforms:

- **Azure Functions**: Event-driven serverless compute
- **Azure Logic Apps**: Orchestrated workflows with connectors
- **Event Hubs**: Streaming downstream for analytics
- **Storage Accounts**: Trigger on blob uploads/deletions
- **Azure Automation, Webhooks, and Power Automate**: For low-code/no-code automation
- **Custom Webhooks**: Push events to any RESTful endpoint

For example, automatically resize images on blob upload:

1. Blob created in images/uploads/

2. System topic triggers Event Grid event
3. Event Grid subscription calls an Azure Function to resize image

This creates a serverless, scalable pipeline with zero polling and minimal latency.

Filtering and Event Routing

Event Grid supports advanced filtering to route events based on:

- Event type (e.g., UserCreated, PaymentProcessed)
- Subject pattern (e.g., /invoices/*)
- Data content (e.g., amount > 1000)

```
"filter": {
"subjectBeginsWith": "/invoices/",
"subjectEndsWith": ".json",
"includedEventTypes": ["InvoiceGenerated"]
}
```

Filters are declarative and do not require modifying event producers, allowing centralized control over routing.

Security and Access Control

Security is enforced via:

- **Shared Access Keys (SAS tokens)** for publishing to custom topics

- **Azure Active Directory (AAD)** for RBAC-based access to manage topics and subscriptions

- **Event validation** for custom webhooks via handshake mechanisms

Best practices include:

- Storing secrets in **Azure Key Vault**

- Limiting topic access via RBAC roles

- Enabling diagnostic logs for auditability

Monitoring and Diagnostics

Event Grid integrates with Azure Monitor for tracking event flow, delivery latency, failures, and throttling.

Common metrics:

- PublishSuccessCount

- PublishFailureCount

- DeliverySuccessCount

- DeliveryFailureCount

Logs can be routed to:

- Azure Log Analytics

- Storage Blob (archival)

- Azure Event Hubs (for real-time analytics)

Monitoring helps detect handler outages, misconfigurations, or excessive retries.

Common Use Cases

1. Resource State Notifications

Track changes to Azure resources (e.g., virtual machine starts, blob deletions) and trigger automation.

2. Reactive Microservices

Enable loose coupling between microservices using event notifications without direct dependencies.

3. File Processing Pipelines

Respond to storage changes (e.g., uploaded documents or media) and process them in a distributed pipeline.

4. Business Events Distribution

Emit custom business events like InvoiceGenerated, UserSignedUp, or OrderShipped to multiple systems.

5. Webhook Integration with SaaS Systems

Bridge Azure apps with third-party services such as Salesforce, Slack, or Stripe through custom events.

Event Grid vs Other Azure Services

Feature	Event Grid	Service Bus	Event Hubs
Delivery Mode	Push	Pull	Pull
Scale	Millions of events/sec	Thousands/sec	Millions/sec
Latency	Low (<100 ms)	Medium	Low
Ordering	Not guaranteed	FIFO with sessions	Per partition
Dead-Lettering	Optional to Blob	Native DLQ	None
Filtering	Yes	Subscription Rules	No
Target Use Case	Notifications, triggers	Workflows, commands	Telemetry, analytics

Cost Model

Event Grid charges based on:

- **Operations** (event ingress and egress)
- **Subscriptions**
- **Advanced features** like dead-lettering

Sample pricing:

- $0.60 per million operations (subject to regional variance)
- First 100,000 ops/month free (as of writing)

Cost optimization tips:

- Batch events where possible
- Minimize fan-out unless needed
- Use filters to avoid unnecessary egress

Summary

Azure Event Grid offers a powerful foundation for building modern, reactive applications that respond in real time to changes in state, resource conditions, and user interactions. With native Azure integration, advanced filtering, low-latency delivery, and serverless-first compatibility, it supports both operational automation and business-critical workflows.

Unlike Service Bus, Event Grid is not a queue but a routing service that excels at decoupling producers and consumers. By understanding its model, strengths, and best practices, you can architect systems that are scalable, loosely coupled, and responsive to the dynamic nature of today's digital ecosystems.

In the next section, we'll examine Azure Event Hubs, the platform designed for massive-scale event ingestion, stream analytics, and telemetry collection.

Azure Event Hubs

Azure Event Hubs is a high-throughput, fully managed data streaming platform and event ingestion service that is capable of receiving and processing millions of events per second. It is designed specifically for large-scale telemetry and log ingestion, enabling the real-time collection and processing of data from a variety of sources such as applications, IoT devices, mobile apps, cloud services, and infrastructure components.

Unlike Azure Service Bus and Event Grid, which are optimized for message handling and lightweight reactive events respectively, Event Hubs is built for massive data ingestion and real-time stream processing. It serves as the front door to big data pipelines, making it foundational to analytics-driven architectures in Azure.

Core Architecture and Concepts

Event Producers

An **event producer** is any application or service that sends data to an Event Hub. These producers can use REST APIs or SDKs to push data into the hub. Common producers include:

- Web applications sending usage data
- IoT devices streaming sensor readings
- Microservices emitting operational logs
- Infrastructure agents exporting metrics

Event producers do not need to know how events are consumed or processed downstream. This decoupling is a key architectural advantage.

```
from azure.eventhub import EventHubProducerClient, EventData

producer = EventHubProducerClient.from_connection_string(conn_str, eventhub_name="telemetry-stream")
```

```
event_data_batch = producer.create_batch()

event_data_batch.add(EventData('{"deviceId": "sensor-001", "temperature": 24.6}'))

producer.send_batch(event_data_batch)
```

This Python snippet demonstrates sending a simple telemetry message to an Event Hub.

Partitions and Throughput

At the heart of Event Hubs is its **partitioned consumer model**. Each Event Hub is divided into multiple **partitions**, which provide:

- **Parallelism**: Events can be consumed in parallel from different partitions.
- **Ordering**: Events within a partition are strictly ordered.
- **Isolation**: High-volume streams do not block or interfere with each other.

You can specify a **partition key** when sending events to ensure that related events (e.g., from the same device) are routed to the same partition, preserving order.

```
producer.sendBatch([{ body: "event-1" }, { body: "event-2" }], { partitionKey: "device-123" });
```

Event Hubs supports **Throughput Units (TUs)** in the Standard tier and **Capacity Units (CUs)** in the Dedicated tier. TUs define ingress and egress bandwidth limits and can be scaled or auto-inflated based on usage.

Consumer Groups

A **consumer group** represents a separate view of the event stream. Multiple consumer groups can read from the same Event Hub independently. This allows different processing pipelines—e.g., analytics, storage, alerting—to work in parallel without interfering with each other.

Each consumer group maintains its own **offsets**, which track the last event consumed from each partition. Offsets can be persisted in Azure Blob Storage, Azure Table Storage, or external systems.

Example: One consumer group sends events to Azure Data Lake for batch analytics; another sends real-time alerts to an operations dashboard.

Event Retention and Replay

Event Hubs retains events for a configurable period—up to **7 days** in the Standard tier and **90 days** in Dedicated. Consumers can replay events from a specific offset, sequence number, or timestamp. This allows for:

- Recovery from consumer failure
- Replaying data for model training
- Running new analytics jobs on old data

You can also **capture** events automatically to Azure Blob Storage or Azure Data Lake using Event Hubs Capture.

{

"enabled": true,

```
"encoding": "Avro",
"intervalInSeconds": 300,
"sizeLimitInBytes": 524288000,
"destination": {
"name": "EventHubArchive",
"properties": {
"storageAccountResourceId": "/subscriptions/.../storageAccounts/mydatalake",
"blobContainer": "event-capture"
}
}
}
```

Captured data can then be queried using Azure Synapse or Azure Data Explorer.

Event Processing and Integration

Event Hubs is built for real-time stream processing. Azure provides several options for consuming and processing events:

Azure Stream Analytics

Stream Analytics enables real-time querying and transformation using SQL-like syntax. It is ideal for detecting patterns, aggregating metrics, and filtering streams.

```
SELECT
deviceId,
AVG(temperature) AS avgTemp
INTO
alertOutput
FROM
telemetryStream TIMESTAMP BY eventTime
GROUP BY
deviceId, TumblingWindow(minute, 5)
HAVING
AVG(temperature) > 30
```

This query detects overheating devices over a rolling 5-minute window.

Azure Functions

Event Hubs can trigger serverless Azure Functions. This enables lightweight, on-demand processing for event-driven use cases.

```
[FunctionName("TelemetryProcessor")]
public static void Run(
[EventHubTrigger("telemetry-stream", Connection = "EventHubConnection")] string[] messages,
ILogger log)
```

```
{
foreach (var message in messages)
log.LogInformation($"Processed message: {message}");
}
```

Function scaling is tied to event volume, providing elasticity for dynamic workloads.

Apache Kafka Compatibility

Event Hubs offers a **Kafka endpoint** so that existing Kafka clients can connect to Event Hubs without changing code. This reduces friction for migrating or integrating with legacy systems using Kafka.

Use cases:

- MirrorMaker2 for Kafka-to-Azure replication
- Confluent applications consuming from Event Hubs
- Kafka clients in Kubernetes emitting logs to Azure

Example connection string:

```
bootstrap.servers=myeventhubnamespace.servicebus.windows.net:9093
security.protocol=SASL_SSL
sasl.mechanism=PLAIN
```

Monitoring and Diagnostics

Azure provides comprehensive telemetry for Event Hubs:

- **Metrics**: Ingress/Egress volume, Throttled Requests, Successful Requests, Capture Errors
- **Logs**: Request logs, client IPs, delivery status
- **Alerts**: High CPU, partition lag, unauthorized access attempts

You can visualize these metrics in Azure Monitor or forward them to Log Analytics and Grafana.

Lag detection is especially important:

- Measures the delay between event enqueue and consumption
- Indicates bottlenecks in downstream processing
- Can be used to auto-scale consumer apps

Security and Access Control

Event Hubs supports multiple layers of security:

- **Shared Access Policies (SAS tokens)** for scoped access
- **Azure AD-based RBAC** for identity-based access control
- **Private Endpoints and VNet Integration** (Premium & Dedicated tiers)
- **Encryption at Rest and in Transit** using Microsoft-managed or customer-managed keys (CMK)

Best practices include:

- Limiting SAS permissions (send/receive/manage)
- Rotating SAS keys periodically
- Using Azure Key Vault for secure secret management
- Enabling diagnostics logs for auditability

Common Use Cases

1. IoT Telemetry Ingestion

Event Hubs is ideal for collecting and processing high-frequency data from sensors, devices, and industrial machines.

2. Application and Infrastructure Logging

Capture logs from applications, Azure services, and third-party systems for analysis, alerting, and storage.

3. Clickstream and Usage Analytics

Web and mobile apps can send user interaction data to Event Hubs for real-time behavioral analysis and personalization.

4. Security Monitoring and Threat Detection

Ingest security logs from firewalls, IDS/IPS systems, and cloud workloads for analysis by SIEM tools.

5. Financial Data Feeds

Stream real-time market data, payment transactions, or fraud signals for high-speed analytics and response.

Cost Model

Pricing is based on:

- **Throughput Units (TUs)** or **Capacity Units (CUs)**
- **Ingress/egress volume**
- **Capture feature usage**
- **Retention duration**

Guidelines:

- 1 TU = 1 MB/sec ingress + 2 MB/sec egress
- Auto-inflate enables scaling without manual intervention
- Capture incurs storage costs based on retention and size

Cost optimization:

- Use batching for efficient ingress
- Tune partition count for load distribution
- Archive older data to cost-effective storage

Event Hubs vs Other Messaging Services

Feature	Event Hubs	Service Bus	Event Grid
Target Use Case	Telemetry, logs	Commands, workflows	Notifications, triggers
Scale	Millions/sec	Thousands/sec	Millions/sec
Delivery Mode	Pull	Pull	Push
Ordering	Per partition	FIFO (with sessions)	Not guaranteed
Retention	Up to 7/90 days	Queue TTL	Up to 24 hrs (retry)
Replay Support	Yes	No	No
Kafka Support	Yes	No	No

Summary

Azure Event Hubs is the backbone of real-time, high-scale data ingestion on Azure. It enables telemetry collection, log aggregation, and stream analytics at cloud scale. With support for partitions, consumer groups, event replay, Kafka compatibility, and real-time processing, Event Hubs is essential for any application that needs to react to continuous streams of data.

By integrating Event Hubs with services like Azure Stream Analytics, Functions, and Synapse, you can build full-stack analytical pipelines that provide insights, trigger workflows, and power intelligent applications. The next sections will explore how to use Azure Storage Queues and compare all messaging options to help you make the right architectural choices.

Azure Storage Queues

Azure Storage Queues provide a simple, durable, and cost-effective queuing solution for decoupling components and enabling asynchronous workflows within cloud applications. As one of the core services in the Azure Storage suite, Storage Queues enable reliable message delivery between distributed application components, microservices, or background workers. While not as feature-rich as Azure Service Bus or optimized for high-scale event ingestion like Event Hubs, Storage Queues are a practical choice for lightweight scenarios where simplicity, cost, and integration with storage services take priority.

This section explores the architecture, features, use cases, limitations, and operational considerations of Azure Storage Queues.

Architecture and Core Concepts

Azure Storage Queues are part of **Azure Storage Accounts** and are backed by Azure's globally distributed, highly available storage platform. Each storage account can host multiple queues, and each queue can contain millions of messages.

A typical queue message lifecycle involves:

1. **Enqueueing**: A producer sends a message to a named queue.
2. **Dequeueing**: A consumer reads and processes a message.
3. **Visibility timeout**: After a message is read, it is hidden temporarily to prevent concurrent processing.
4. **Deletion**: If the message is successfully processed, the consumer deletes it from the queue.

If not deleted within the visibility timeout, the message becomes visible again and can be retried by another consumer.

Key Properties:

- Maximum message size: **64 KB** (base tier)
- Message TTL (Time-To-Live): **up to 7 days**
- Maximum queue length: **unbounded**, subject to account limits
- Delivery model: **At-least-once**, FIFO not guaranteed
- Protocols: **REST API, Azure SDKs, Azure CLI**

Creating and Using Storage Queues

You must first provision a **Storage Account**, then create a queue within that account. Messages are base64-encoded and stored as individual records.

```
resource storageAccount 'Microsoft.Storage/storageAccounts@2023-01-01' = {

name: 'myqueueappstore'

location: 'West Europe'

sku: {

name: 'Standard_LRS'

}

kind: 'StorageV2'
```

```
}

resource queue 'Microsoft.Storage/storageAccounts/queueServices/queues@2023-01-01' = {

name: '${storageAccount.name}/default/email-queue'

}
```

Once created, the queue can be accessed using the Azure SDK:

```
var queueClient = new QueueClient(connectionString, "email-queue");

await queueClient.CreateIfNotExistsAsync();

await queueClient.SendMessageAsync("Send welcome email to user@example.com");
```

Message Retrieval and Processing

When a consumer retrieves a message, it becomes invisible to other consumers for a configurable **visibility timeout** period. If proccssing fails, the message becomes visible again after the timeout and can be retried.

```
QueueMessage[] messages = await queueClient.ReceiveMessagesAsync(maxMessages: 1, visibilityTimeout: TimeSpan.FromSeconds(30));

foreach (QueueMessage message in messages)

{

ProcessMessage(message.MessageText);
```

```
await queueClient.DeleteMessageAsync(message.MessageId,
message.PopReceipt);

}
```

This pull-based model simplifies concurrency control and fault handling.

Use Cases

Azure Storage Queues are suited to a variety of lightweight messaging scenarios, particularly where advanced broker features (like sessions, transactions, or filtering) are not required.

1. Background Job Processing

A web app can enqueue tasks (e.g., sending emails, generating reports) to be processed by background workers independently.

2. Decoupling Microservices

Storage Queues help decouple service-to-service communication, allowing services to function independently of each other's availability.

3. Retryable Task Handling

Failed messages can be retried automatically after visibility timeout. Developers can implement exponential backoff and poison message handling with custom logic.

4. Cost-Conscious Workloads

For low-frequency, low-complexity systems, Storage Queues provide a significantly cheaper alternative to Service Bus queues.

5. Integration with Azure Functions

Azure Functions can be triggered by Storage Queue messages with minimal setup. This supports scalable and event-driven architectures.

```
[FunctionName("EmailQueueProcessor")]

public async Task Run([QueueTrigger("email-queue", Connection = "AzureWebJobsStorage")] string message, ILogger log)

{

log.LogInformation($"Processing email task: {message}");

}
```

Comparison with Azure Service Bus Queues

Feature	Storage Queues	Service Bus Queues
Message Size Limit	64 KB	256 KB / 1 MB (Premium)
Delivery Guarantee	At-least-once	At-least-once + deduplication
Ordering	Not guaranteed	FIFO via sessions
Dead-Letter Queue (DLQ)	Manual implementation	Built-in DLQ
Message TTL	Up to 7 days	Configurable per queue/ message
Encryption at Rest	Yes	Yes
Pricing	Very low	Higher (based on operations)
Advanced Features	None	Sessions, Transactions, Filters

Limitations

Despite their utility, Storage Queues have notable limitations:

- **No native dead-lettering**: You must implement your own DLQ mechanism.
- **No advanced filtering**: All consumers must retrieve and inspect all messages.
- **No guaranteed ordering**: Even if messages are enqueued in order, concurrent processing may reorder them.

- **Low throughput**: Better suited for low to medium traffic compared to Event Hubs.

- **Limited analytics integration**: No direct stream analytics or Kafka-style interfaces.

These constraints make Storage Queues less appropriate for enterprise-scale, event-sourced, or transactional messaging patterns.

Security and Access Control

Access to Storage Queues is governed via:

- **Shared Access Signatures (SAS tokens)**

- **Storage Account Keys**

- **Azure AD integration** (with RBAC for data plane access)

- **Private Endpoints and VNet integration** for network isolation

Best practices include:

- Enabling logging via **Storage Analytics**

- Using **Azure Key Vault** to manage access keys and secrets

- Auditing access via **Azure Monitor Diagnostic Settings**

Monitoring and Diagnostics

Storage Queues integrate with Azure Monitor and provide metrics including:

- QueueMessageCount: Number of visible messages
- QueueCapacity: Used and available storage
- Ingress / Egress Bytes: Throughput measurements

Queue metrics help with:

- Auto-scaling consumers based on queue length
- Alerting on backlog or deadlock conditions
- Forecasting workload trends

Example: Create an alert when QueueMessageCount exceeds 1000.

```
resource alert 'Microsoft.Insights/metricAlerts@2018-03-01' = {
name: 'QueueBacklogAlert'
location: 'global'
properties: {
severity: 2
enabled: true
scopes: [queue.id]
evaluationFrequency: 'PT5M'
windowSize: 'PT5M'
```

```
criteria: {
allOf: [
{
metricName: 'QueueMessageCount'
timeAggregation: 'Average'
operator: 'GreaterThan'
threshold: 1000
}
]
}
actions: []
}
}
```

Cost Considerations

Storage Queues are extremely cost-effective:

- You pay per **transaction** (enqueue, dequeue, peek)
- No charges for idle time or retained messages
- Integrated under the broader **Azure Storage pricing** tier

They are ideal for cost-sensitive workloads, prototypes, or applications with infrequent traffic.

Cost optimization tips:

- Batch read/write operations when possible
- Delete processed messages promptly
- Use lifecycle management to archive/expire unused queues

Best Practices

To maximize reliability and maintainability:

- **Use unique message IDs** for idempotency
- **Persist message processing status** in durable storage
- **Implement exponential backoff** for retries
- **Use queue length metrics** for consumer autoscaling
- **Log poison messages** for offline analysis

For example, failed messages can be moved to a separate "poison-queue" after multiple failed processing attempts, creating a manual DLQ.

Summary

Azure Storage Queues provide a simple, resilient, and cost-efficient messaging solution for lightweight scenarios. While lacking advanced messaging constructs like ordering, dead-lettering, and transactions, they are ideal for straightforward producer-consumer models, decoupling services, or powering background jobs.

With native support in Azure Functions, integration with the Storage ecosystem, and pay-as-you-go pricing, Storage Queues offer a compelling option for developers seeking to build scalable yet minimal overhead cloud applications.

In the final section of this chapter, we'll compare all four Azure messaging services and explore guidelines for selecting the right one based on use case, performance, and architectural requirements.

Comparative Scenarios: Choosing the Right Service

Choosing the appropriate Azure messaging service is a critical architectural decision that can significantly impact system scalability, performance, cost, reliability, and maintainability. Azure offers four core messaging and event services—**Service Bus**, **Event Grid**, **Event Hubs**, and **Storage Queues**—each designed for specific workloads and usage patterns.

This section presents a comprehensive comparison of these services across multiple dimensions, explores common architectural scenarios, and provides actionable guidance to help architects and developers select the best-fit solution for each use case.

Comparison Matrix

Feature	Azure Service Bus	Azure Event Grid	Azure Event Hubs	Azure Storage Queues
Primary Use Case	Enterprise messaging, workflows	Lightweight eventing	Telemetry/ event ingestion	Simple decoupling, background jobs
Delivery Model	Pull-based	Push-based	Pull-based	Pull-based
Message Size Limit	256 KB (Standard), 1 MB (Premium)	1 MB	1 MB	64 KB
FIFO Support	Yes (via sessions)	No	Yes (per partition)	No
Exactly Once Processing	Yes (with duplication detection)	No	No	No
Retention	TTL-based	24 hours max	Up to 7–90 days	Up to 7 days
Dead-Letter Queue	Built-in	Optional (via blob)	No	Manual
Ordering Guarantees	Yes (via sessions)	No	Per-partition only	No
Filtering and Routing	SQL filters (topics)	Event type/ subject filters	Not available	Not available
Fan-out Support	Topics with multiple subs	Native	Multiple consumers/	Manual

			groups	
Throughput	Moderate	High	Very High	Low to Moderate
Azure Functions Integration	Yes	Yes	Yes	Yes
Cost	Moderate to High (Premium)	Low	Moderate	Very Low
Network Isolation	Premium with VNet support	Private endpoints available	Private link (Dedicated tier)	VNet with private endpoint
Kafka Protocol Support	No	No	Yes	No

Decision Factors and Recommendations

1. Type of Communication

- **Command-based Messaging (Imperative):**
  - Use **Azure Service Bus**
  - Example: "Process payment", "Ship order"
  - Requires reliable delivery, ordering, and workflows
- **Event Notification (Declarative):**
  - Use **Azure Event Grid**
  - Example: "File uploaded", "User signed up"

  ○ Ideal for loose coupling, push notifications, and automation

- **High-Frequency Telemetry:**

  ○ Use **Azure Event Hubs**

  ○ Example: IoT sensors, log aggregation, clickstream data

  ○ Designed for massive parallel ingestion and stream processing

- **Simple Task Queuing:**

  ○ Use **Azure Storage Queues**

  ○ Example: Email dispatch, file conversion, background jobs

  ○ Lightweight and cost-effective with minimal operational overhead

2. Scalability Needs

- **Event Hubs** supports millions of events/sec with partitions and consumer groups.

- **Event Grid** delivers events with sub-second latency and high throughput.

- **Service Bus Premium** can scale reliably but with more overhead.

- **Storage Queues** are best for low to moderate scale; throughput is limited.

Use **auto-scaling consumers** and **partitioning** for high-volume ingestion with Event Hubs. Use **topics** and **subscriptions** for load distribution in Service Bus.

3. Message Durability and Replay

- **Event Hubs** provides event replay via offsets and sequence numbers.
- **Service Bus** provides durable storage, with dead-lettering and message deferral.
- **Event Grid** does not support replay—focus is on real-time notification.
- **Storage Queues** offer basic message retention with TTL, no replay support.

Use Event Hubs for streaming scenarios where auditability and replay are crucial (e.g., machine learning pipelines). Use Service Bus when durable, transactional message processing is required.

4. Latency Sensitivity

- **Event Grid**: Sub-second latency, ideal for near real-time notifications.
- **Event Hubs**: Low latency with batch delivery.
- **Service Bus**: Slightly higher latency due to transactional guarantees.
- **Storage Queues**: Moderate latency; visibility timeout may introduce delays.

For push-based, low-latency event delivery, Event Grid is optimal. For scenarios where latency is acceptable but delivery guarantees are paramount, use Service Bus.

5. Security and Isolation Requirements

- **Service Bus Premium** supports private endpoints and full VNet isolation.
- **Event Grid** supports private endpoints and managed identities.
- **Event Hubs** supports private link in Dedicated tier.
- **Storage Queues** can be secured via private endpoints and RBAC.

Choose Premium tiers when isolation and compliance are mandatory, such as in finance, healthcare, or government workloads.

6. Developer Complexity and Integration

- **Event Grid** offers simple webhook integration and requires minimal setup.
- **Storage Queues** are easy to use and integrate well with Azure Functions.
- **Service Bus** provides a robust API with advanced features, requiring deeper knowledge.
- **Event Hubs** requires understanding of partitions and offsets for consumption.

Choose simplicity with Event Grid and Storage Queues for smaller applications. Use Service Bus or Event Hubs for production-scale workflows and telemetry pipelines.

Scenario-Based Recommendations

Scenario 1: Processing Orders with Business Workflow

- **Need**: Reliable, transactional, sequential message handling
- **Service**: Azure Service Bus
- **Rationale**: Supports sessions, dead-lettering, ordering, and transactional workflows

Scenario 2: Event Notification from Blob Uploads

- **Need**: React to blob creation to trigger processing
- **Service**: Azure Event Grid
- **Rationale**: Native support for Blob Storage events, push-based routing to Functions or Logic Apps

Scenario 3: Ingesting IoT Telemetry from Thousands of Devices

- **Need**: High-throughput, time-ordered ingestion with replay capability
- **Service**: Azure Event Hubs
- **Rationale**: Partitioned ingestion, multiple consumers, supports stream analytics

Scenario 4: Low-Cost Background Job Queue

- **Need**: Simple, low-frequency message dispatch with durability
- **Service**: Azure Storage Queues
- **Rationale**: Easy integration, low cost, basic queuing needs only

Scenario 5: Multi-Consumer Event Routing

- **Need**: Send business events to analytics, alerts, and audit services
- **Service**: Event Grid with multiple subscriptions
- **Rationale**: Built-in fan-out, routing filters, and low latency

Scenario 6: Hybrid System with Commands and Events

- **Need**: Combine imperative commands with reactive events
- **Service**: Use Service Bus for commands and Event Grid for events
- **Rationale**: Clear separation of control flow and data change signaling

Integration with Azure Functions and Logic Apps

All messaging services integrate with **Azure Functions**, allowing serverless processing of messages and events.

Trigger Type	Service Integration
QueueTrigger	Storage Queues
ServiceBusTrigger	Service Bus (queue/topic)
EventHubTrigger	Event Hubs
EventGridTrigger	Event Grid

Logic Apps also support these services as both triggers and actions, making it ideal for no-code automation and workflows across multiple systems.

Cost Optimization Strategies

- **Batching** messages where supported (Event Hubs, Service Bus)
- **Using TTL** to expire stale messages
- **Filtering events** to reduce delivery volume (Event Grid)
- **Choosing the right tier** based on feature needs (e.g., Basic vs Premium)
- **Auto-scaling consumers** to match event volume
- **Archiving old data** from Event Hubs to cold storage via Capture

Summary

Each Azure messaging service is optimized for a different class of problem:

- Use **Service Bus** for enterprise-grade messaging, workflows, and guaranteed delivery.
- Use **Event Grid** for reactive, lightweight, real-time notifications.
- Use **Event Hubs** for ingesting and processing large-scale streaming data.
- Use **Storage Queues** for simple, durable message queuing in cost-sensitive workloads.

Understanding the distinctions between these services, and how they fit into architectural patterns such as event-driven design, microservices, telemetry pipelines, and decoupled systems, empowers architects and developers to build robust, scalable, and efficient solutions.

In the next chapter, we will explore architectural best practices for designing real-time solutions using these messaging services, with a focus on performance, security, scalability, and cloud-native design principles.

Chapter 4: Designing Real-Time Solutions with Azure

Architectural Patterns for Real-Time Applications

Designing real-time systems requires a fundamentally different mindset than traditional batch or request-response architectures. Real-time solutions are inherently dynamic, event-driven, scalable, and asynchronous. They must be designed to process and react to incoming data streams or events as they occur—often at scale, across distributed systems, and within strict latency budgets.

Azure provides a broad and powerful set of messaging services (Service Bus, Event Grid, Event Hubs, Storage Queues) that enable the implementation of modern real-time architectural patterns. In this section, we explore key patterns for building cloud-native real-time applications, their applicability in Azure, and how to architect them effectively for high performance, reliability, and maintainability.

1. Event-Driven Architecture (EDA)

At the heart of real-time design is **Event-Driven Architecture (EDA)**—a style in which systems communicate by producing and consuming discrete events. Events represent facts (e.g., "OrderPlaced") rather than commands, allowing for loose coupling between producers and consumers.

Key Benefits:

- Decoupling: Producers and consumers evolve independently.

- Scalability: Consumers can be scaled horizontally.
- Flexibility: New consumers can be added without changing producers.

Azure Implementation:

- Use **Event Grid** for lightweight events with broad fan-out.
- Use **Event Hubs** for high-throughput event streaming (telemetry).
- Use **Service Bus Topics** for structured pub/sub messaging.

Example:

A logistics platform emits an OrderShipped event via Event Grid. Downstream consumers include:

- Notification service (emails the user)
- Billing system (triggers invoice)
- Analytics platform (tracks delivery trends)

Each consumer acts independently, increasing system modularity.

2. CQRS (Command Query Responsibility Segregation)

CQRS separates write operations (commands) from read operations (queries), allowing for independently optimized data models, scalability, and performance characteristics.

In real-time systems, this often pairs with event sourcing to rebuild query models from a sequence of events.

Pattern Overview:

- **Command Side**: Issues state-changing operations (e.g., create user)
- **Query Side**: Serves read-optimized views (e.g., user profiles)

Azure Implementation:

- Commands are sent through **Service Bus Queues**
- State changes emit events via **Event Grid**
- Read models are materialized in **Cosmos DB**, **Azure SQL**, or **Azure Search**

```
// Command handler
await serviceBusSender.SendMessageAsync(new ServiceBusMessage(JsonSerializer.Serialize(createOrderCommand)));
// Event emitter
await eventGridClient.PublishEventsAsync("orders-topic", new List<EventGridEvent> {
new EventGridEvent("orders/order123", "OrderCreated", "1.0", eventData)
});
```

Use Case:

A banking app processes a fund transfer command. Once validated and persisted, it emits an event. The read model is updated and can be queried immediately, separate from the transactional logic.

3. Event Sourcing

Event sourcing persists application state as a series of immutable events rather than current state snapshots. Each change to the application state is captured as an event and stored in an append-only log.

Advantages:

- Complete audit trail
- Supports replay for recovery or new projections
- Enables temporal queries and debugging

Azure Implementation:

- Use **Event Hubs** or **Service Bus** to store events
- Store event log in **Cosmos DB**, **Azure Blob Storage**, or **Data Lake**
- Use **Stream Analytics** or **Azure Functions** to process and project events

Example:

A stock trading app stores every action—order placed, order executed, position closed—as an event. Users can view portfolio state at any historical point by replaying events.

[

{ "eventType": "OrderPlaced", "data": { "orderId": "O123" } },

{ "eventType": "OrderExecuted", "data": { "orderId": "O123" } }

]

4. Pub/Sub Messaging

Publish/Subscribe (pub/sub) decouples senders from receivers by introducing topics and subscriptions. A publisher sends messages to a topic, and multiple independent subscribers receive relevant messages based on filters or routing logic.

Azure Implementation:

- Use **Service Bus Topics** for structured pub/sub with filtering
- Use **Event Grid** for lightweight event distribution to many consumers

Example:

An HR system publishes EmployeePromoted events. Subscribers include:

- Payroll service (adjusts salary)
- IT team (upgrades access)
- Facilities (changes office allocation)

```
resource topic 'Microsoft.ServiceBus/namespaces/topics@2022-10-01-preview' = {

name: 'employee-events'
```

```
parent: sbNamespace

}

resource promotionSub 'Microsoft.ServiceBus/namespaces/topics/subscriptions@2022-10-01-preview' = {

name: 'payroll-service-sub'

parent: topic

properties: {

filter: {

sqlExpression: "eventType = 'EmployeePromoted'"

}

}

}
```

5. Stream Processing

Stream processing deals with continuous ingestion and transformation of data in motion. Rather than storing data for later analysis, data is processed and acted upon immediately.

Azure Tools:

- **Event Hubs** for ingestion
- **Azure Stream Analytics** for real-time SQL-based processing
- **Azure Functions** for event-driven transformations

Common Use Cases:

- Fraud detection in payment systems
- Monitoring application logs for anomalies
- Aggregating IoT sensor data into dashboards

Example:

```
SELECT

sensorId,

COUNT(*) AS errorCount

INTO

alerts

FROM

inputStream TIMESTAMP BY eventTime

WHERE

status = 'error'

GROUP BY

sensorId, TumblingWindow(minute, 5)

HAVING

COUNT(*) > 10
```

This real-time query detects sensors failing repeatedly within 5-minute windows.

6. Backpressure and Load Leveling

Backpressure occurs when producers send messages faster than consumers can process. Load leveling introduces buffers (e.g., queues) to smoothen spikes.

Azure Implementation:

- Use **Service Bus Queues** or **Storage Queues** as buffers
- Set **max delivery count** and **lock duration** to throttle retries
- Monitor queue depth to auto-scale consumers

Example:

A retail platform receives thousands of orders per minute during a flash sale. Service Bus queues handle the burst while worker services consume at steady pace.

```
var receiver = client.CreateReceiver("order-queue", new ServiceBusReceiverOptions {
PrefetchCount = 20
});
```

7. Choreography vs. Orchestration

- **Orchestration**: Centralized workflow engine controls process execution (e.g., Durable Functions, Logic Apps)
- **Choreography**: Components emit and react to events in a decentralized fashion

Choreography promotes scalability and autonomy. Azure Event Grid and Event Hubs are ideal for choreographed systems.

Orchestration is better when processes must follow a defined sequence. Use Azure **Durable Functions** or **Logic Apps**.

Example:

A travel booking app orchestrates flight, hotel, and car bookings using Durable Functions. A payment failure cancels all bookings. Alternatively, services can independently react to BookingConfirmed event using choreography.

8. Saga Pattern

A **Saga** is a sequence of local transactions coordinated via events. It provides a way to manage distributed transactions in eventually consistent systems.

Azure Implementation:

- Trigger services via **Event Grid**
- Compensate failed transactions via **Service Bus**
- Use **Stateful Durable Functions** to track saga state

Example:

- Step 1: Debit user account
- Step 2: Reserve inventory
- Step 3: Ship product

If inventory reservation fails, compensate by refunding the account.

9. Lambda Architecture for Real-Time + Batch

Lambda architecture combines **batch processing** of historical data and **stream processing** of real-time data.

Azure Services:

- Batch: Azure Data Lake + Azure Synapse
- Speed layer: Event Hubs + Stream Analytics
- Serving layer: Azure SQL, Cosmos DB, or Power BI

Use Case:

Analyzing customer behavior in real time while running nightly ETL jobs on historical data.

Summary

Designing real-time applications in Azure involves understanding and applying a variety of cloud-native architectural patterns. From event-driven systems and pub/sub messaging to CQRS, event sourcing, and stream analytics, each pattern serves a specific set of needs and constraints.

Choosing the right combination of patterns and Azure services is key to delivering scalable, resilient, and maintainable solutions. In subsequent sections, we'll examine deeper implementations of these patterns—starting with CQRS and event sourcing in the context of Azure's messaging ecosystem. We'll also explore how to secure, scale, and optimize these real-time solutions for production workloads.

Event Sourcing and CQRS with Azure

Event Sourcing and Command Query Responsibility Segregation (CQRS) are two architectural patterns that complement each other particularly well in real-time and distributed system design. While each can be applied independently, their combined application provides a robust approach to building systems that are highly scalable, auditable, and responsive. Azure provides the foundational building blocks to implement these patterns effectively at enterprise scale.

This section explores the principles, design approaches, implementation strategies, and real-world applications of Event Sourcing and CQRS using Azure's messaging, compute, and storage services.

Understanding Event Sourcing

Event Sourcing is an architectural pattern in which the state of an application is determined by a sequence of immutable events, rather than being stored as the current state in a relational model. Each event captures a specific change in the state of an entity.

Instead of performing CRUD operations directly on entities, the application persists the events that lead to those changes. The current state is then derived by replaying these events in order.

Example Event Stream:

1. UserRegistered { userId: 'U001', name: 'Alice' }

2. UserEmailUpdated { userId: 'U001', newEmail: 'alice@example.com' }

3. UserPromoted { userId: 'U001', newRole: 'Manager' }

The resulting user profile is inferred by applying these events sequentially.

Key Advantages:

- Full audit trail and traceability
- Ability to reconstruct past states (temporal queries)
- Natural support for distributed event-driven systems
- Simplifies replication and integration via event streams

Azure Implementation:

- Use **Azure Event Hubs** or **Azure Service Bus Topics** for appending event logs
- Persist events to **Azure Cosmos DB**, **Azure Blob Storage**, or **Data Lake**
- Use **Azure Functions** or **Stream Analytics** to derive projections (read models)

```
{
"eventId": "e123",
"type": "UserRegistered",
"timestamp": "2025-05-09T12:00:00Z",
"data": {
"userId": "U001",
```

"name": "Alice"

}

}

This event could be stored as a JSON document and used to derive the current state of the user object.

Understanding CQRS

CQRS (Command Query Responsibility Segregation) is a pattern that splits a system's read and write operations into separate models:

- **Commands** mutate the system's state and are handled by the **write model**
- **Queries** retrieve data and are served by the **read model**, which is often denormalized for performance

By separating reads and writes, CQRS provides several benefits:

- Independent scaling of read and write workloads
- Optimized storage structures per use case (OLAP vs. OLTP)
- Enables eventual consistency and better performance in distributed systems

Event Sourcing + CQRS in Practice

When combined:

- Commands result in events that are stored in an event store
- Events are projected into read models (materialized views) used by queries

This architecture supports reactive systems where changes propagate as streams, and where components can evolve independently.

Azure Architecture Overview

1. **Command API** receives intent from clients
2. **Service Bus Queue** accepts and buffers commands
3. **Command Handlers** process commands and publish events to Event Grid/Event Hubs
4. **Event Store** persists raw immutable events (e.g., Cosmos DB or Blob)
5. **Projector Functions** subscribe to event streams and update read models
6. **Read APIs** query denormalized views (e.g., Cosmos DB, SQL Database, or Search)

Implementing CQRS on Azure

Command Side

Commands are received by APIs or message queues and processed by command handlers. Each command must:

- Validate input
- Verify current state (from snapshot or projection)

- Emit one or more events

Use **Service Bus** for durability and transactional support.

```
public async Task Handle(RegisterUserCommand command)

{

var userRegistered = new UserRegisteredEvent(command.UserId, command.Name, command.Email);

await _eventPublisher.PublishAsync(userRegistered);

}
```

Event Publishing

Events are sent to Event Hubs or Event Grid for downstream processing.

```
var eventData = new EventData(Encoding.UTF8.GetBytes(JsonConvert.SerializeObject(@e

await _eventHubProducer.SendAsync(new[] { eventData });
```

Ensure each event has a unique ID and timestamp for traceability and ordering.

Event Storage

Events should be persisted immutably. Options include:

- **Azure Cosmos DB**: Flexible schema, global distribution
- **Azure Data Lake**: Cost-effective long-term storage

- **Azure Table Storage**: Key-value schema for high write throughput

```
{
"partitionKey": "User_U001",
"rowKey": "2025-05-09T12:00:00Z_e123",
"eventType": "UserRegistered",
"data": { "name": "Alice", "email": "alice@example.com" }
}
```

Use partition keys based on entity identifiers for ordered event grouping.

Implementing Read Models

Events are processed and projected into read-optimized models by dedicated consumers, often Azure Functions.

```
[FunctionName("ProjectUser")]
public async Task Run(
[EventHubTrigger("user-events", Connection = "EventHubConnection")] string[] events,
[CosmosDB("UserDb", "Profiles", Connection = "CosmosConnection")] IAsyncCollector<UserProfile> output)
{
foreach (var e in events)
{
```

```
var evt =
JsonConvert.DeserializeObject<UserRegisteredEvent>(e);

await output.AddAsync(new UserProfile {

Id = evt.UserId,

Name = evt.Name,

Email = evt.Email

});

}

}
```

Read models can be stored in:

- **Cosmos DB** for low-latency global reads
- **SQL Database** for reporting and BI
- **Azure Search** for indexed full-text search

Handling Consistency

CQRS + Event Sourcing naturally leads to **eventual consistency** between the write and read sides. The delay is usually sub-second, but clients must tolerate stale reads.

For operations requiring immediate consistency (e.g., authentication), direct reads from the write model or a snapshot layer may be required.

Error Handling and Retries

Robust implementations must handle:

- **Poison events**: Send to a dead-letter queue for inspection
- **Retry logic**: Use exponential backoff in Azure Functions
- **Duplicate events**: Ensure idempotent event processing using event IDs or hashes

```
—Idempotent UPSERT in SQL

MERGE INTO UserProfiles AS target

USING (SELECT @UserId AS UserId, @Name AS Name) AS source

ON target.UserId = source.UserId

WHEN MATCHED THEN UPDATE SET Name = source.Name

WHEN NOT MATCHED THEN INSERT (UserId, Name) VALUES (source.UserId, source.Name);
```

Auditability and Compliance

Because all changes are captured as events, you gain complete traceability for compliance, auditing, and debugging. Regulatory requirements such as GDPR, HIPAA, or SOX can be addressed with event logs and snapshot archival.

Use Case Examples

E-commerce Platform

- Commands: PlaceOrder, CancelOrder, RefundOrder
- Events: OrderPlaced, OrderCancelled, OrderRefunded
- Read models: OrderHistory (Cosmos DB), SalesDashboard (SQL)

Banking Application

- Commands: InitiateTransfer, AuthorizeTransfer
- Events: TransferInitiated, TransferAuthorized, TransferFailed
- Read models: AccountBalance (Cosmos DB), TransferLedger (Blob)

SaaS Multi-Tenant System

- Commands: CreateTenant, AssignUser, ConfigureFeatures
- Events: TenantCreated, UserAssigned
- Read models: TenantCatalog, FeatureMatrix

Testing Strategies

Test each layer independently:

- **Unit test** command and event handlers
- **Integration test** projection logic with real event streams
- **Contract test** between producers and consumers

Tools:

- Azure Storage Emulator for Cosmos/Queue testing
- Azure Functions Core Tools for local function testing
- Playwright or Cypress for UI interactions with read models

Summary

Combining Event Sourcing with CQRS enables powerful, scalable, and auditable systems that align with modern distributed and event-driven design. Azure provides the services to support every stage of this architecture—from durable message ingestion and event streaming to storage, processing, and projection.

By designing for immutability, separation of concerns, and asynchronous workflows, systems can achieve high availability, rapid feature development, and operational transparency. In the next section, we will focus on optimizing scalability and performance in these real-time designs, ensuring that they continue to operate effectively under load and at scale.

Scalability and Performance Optimization

Designing scalable and performant real-time systems on Azure requires careful consideration of architecture, message flow, service limits, and operational strategies. Scalability is not just about handling large volumes of messages but doing so while maintaining low latency, high availability, and predictable costs. Azure's messaging services—Service Bus, Event Grid, Event Hubs, and Storage Queues—each offer scalability features that can be tuned for optimal performance.

This section provides an in-depth guide on how to build systems that scale horizontally and vertically, how to mitigate bottlenecks, and how to architect messaging flows for peak throughput and responsiveness across various Azure services.

Dimensions of Scalability

Before diving into optimizations, it's important to distinguish between key dimensions of scalability:

- **Throughput**: The volume of messages processed per unit of time (e.g., events per second).
- **Latency**: The delay between event generation and processing.
- **Concurrency**: Number of parallel message handlers or consumers.
- **Durability**: Ability to persist messages during spikes or failures.
- **Elasticity**: Capability to scale resources up/down based on demand.
- **Fan-out**: Ability to deliver a single message to multiple consumers.

Each Azure messaging service provides unique tools and settings to manage these characteristics.

Azure Service Bus Optimization

Azure Service Bus supports queues and topics that provide FIFO, message sessions, and dead-lettering. To scale effectively:

1. Use the Premium Tier

- Premium tier offers **dedicated throughput** units (Messaging Units) that scale independently.
- It supports **VNet integration**, **zones**, and **private endpoints**, reducing network latency and securing message flow.
- Avoid the Standard tier for high-scale workloads due to shared resources and throttling.

2. Partitioned Entities

Partitioned queues and topics distribute messages across multiple fragments within Azure's infrastructure, increasing throughput and reliability.

```
properties: {
enablePartitioning: true
}
```

Use partitioning for workloads exceeding 1,000 messages/sec or requiring higher availability.

3. Prefetch and Batching

Use **prefetching** to retrieve multiple messages in one call, reducing network overhead.

```
var receiver = client.CreateReceiver("orders", new ServiceBusReceiverOptions {
PrefetchCount = 100
});
```

Batching messages during send operations also reduces transaction count and boosts performance.

4. Session Handling

Sessions preserve FIFO order per message group but limit parallelism. For higher throughput, balance session usage with multiple consumers, each handling different sessions concurrently.

5. Message Size

Minimize message size to increase throughput. Consider storing large payloads in **Blob Storage** and passing the URI in the message.

Azure Event Grid Optimization

Azure Event Grid is a push-based, reactive messaging service with ultra-low latency and high fan-out. It is designed for real-time notifications and event-driven automation.

1. Event Filtering

Apply filters to subscriptions to reduce unnecessary event deliveries.

```
"filter": {
"includedEventTypes": ["InvoiceGenerated"],
"subjectBeginsWith": "/invoices/"
}
```

Filtering reduces consumer load, network usage, and cost.

2. Destination Performance

Ensure destination endpoints (e.g., Azure Functions, Logic Apps) can scale with event rate:

- Functions should use **Premium Plan** or **Elastic Premium** for concurrency.
- Logic Apps can be scaled using **parallelism control**.

3. Dead-lettering and Retries

Enable **dead-lettering** to prevent event loss due to transient failures. Configure **retry policies** to account for network hiccups.

```
deadLetterDestination: {
endpointType: 'StorageBlob',
properties: {
resourceId: '/subscriptions/.../storageAccounts/mydlq',
```

```
blobContainerName: 'eventgrid-deadletter'
}
}
```

4. Avoid Event Loops

Prevent circular triggers between services (e.g., Blob → Function → Blob → Event Grid) by using filters or separate topics for internal events.

Azure Event Hubs Optimization

Azure Event Hubs is built for high-throughput event ingestion (millions of events per second) and is ideal for telemetry, logs, and IoT data.

1. Partitioning Strategy

Choose an appropriate **partition count**. Start with a power-of-two value based on anticipated parallel consumers.

- Each partition supports ordered processing.
- Choose a **partition key** (e.g., device ID) to ensure related events land in the same partition.

```
producer.SendAsync(events, new SendOptions {
PartitionKey = "device-001"
});
```

2. Auto-Inflate

Enable **Auto-Inflate** to dynamically increase throughput units (TUs) as needed.

```
properties: {

isAutoInflateEnabled: true

maximumThroughputUnits: 40

}
```

3. Capture Feature

Enable **Event Hubs Capture** to offload data automatically to Blob or Data Lake for batch analytics and avoid bottlenecks in consumers.

```
"captureDescription": {

"enabled": true,

"destination": {

"name": "EventHubArchive",

"properties": {

"storageAccountResourceId": "...",

"blobContainer": "capture"

}

}

}
```

4. Consumer Groups and Checkpointing

Use **multiple consumer groups** for independent processing pipelines (e.g., one for analytics, one for alerts).

Implement **checkpointing** (via Azure Blob Storage or Cosmos DB) to track progress and enable resume-on-failure.

Azure Storage Queues Optimization

Azure Storage Queues are best for low-to-medium throughput tasks. Still, there are optimization techniques:

1. Message Visibility Timeout

Set appropriate **visibility timeout** to allow for retry of unprocessed messages while avoiding duplicate processing.

2. Batch Processing

Use ReceiveMessagesAsync with maxMessages to pull messages in bulk.

```
var messages = await queueClient.ReceiveMessagesAsync(maxMessages: 32);
```

Batch deletion and processing reduce transaction cost.

3. Poison Message Handling

Implement a **custom dead-letter queue** by moving failed messages to a separate queue after N attempts.

4. Queue Length Monitoring

Monitor ApproximateMessageCount to auto-scale workers based on backlog.

Cross-Service Best Practices

1. Async and Idempotent Processing

Design all consumers to be **asynchronous** and **idempotent**:

- Idempotency ensures safe retries.
- Async processing allows higher concurrency.

```
if (!await repository.HasProcessedAsync(eventId))

{

await ProcessEventAsync(event);

await repository.MarkAsProcessedAsync(eventId);

}
```

2. Use Durable and Serverless Compute

- Use **Azure Functions (Premium Plan)** or **App Services** with auto-scale.
- Consider **Durable Functions** for orchestration and fan-out/fan-in patterns.

3. Monitor and Alert on Bottlenecks

Use **Azure Monitor** to track:

- Queue depth
- Throttled operations
- Processing duration
- Function cold starts

Set alerts to detect anomalies and trigger auto-scaling actions.

4. Optimize Network Latency

- Deploy compute close to the messaging service region.
- Use **private endpoints** and **VNet integration** to reduce network hops.
- For latency-sensitive apps, consider **Availability Zones** for isolation and performance.

Sample Auto-Scaling Strategy (Functions + Event Hubs)

1. Enable Event Hub trigger for Azure Function.

2. Choose Premium plan or App Service Plan with scaling enabled.

3. Configure scale-out conditions in Azure Monitor based on:

- IncomingBytes in Event Hubs
- FunctionExecutionCount
- QueueMessageCount

This ensures your function app scales horizontally as event volume grows.

Cost Efficiency Tips

- **Batch messages** during send and receive
- **Expire stale messages** using TTL
- **Filter events** to reduce volume
- **Capture data** for offline analytics rather than duplicating streams
- **Auto-scale consumers** based on metrics

Summary

Scalability and performance in real-time systems are not achieved through brute force but through thoughtful design, service-specific tuning, and continuous monitoring. Each Azure messaging service—Service Bus, Event Grid, Event Hubs, Storage Queues—has unique strengths, configurations, and tuning parameters.

By applying the strategies outlined here, you can build systems that gracefully handle surges in demand, minimize latency, maximize throughput, and operate reliably in production. The next section will address security best practices, ensuring that your real-time messaging infrastructure is not only fast and scalable but also protected against modern threats.

Security Best Practices

Security is a foundational requirement for designing real-time solutions in Azure, especially when handling sensitive data or operating in regulated environments. Real-time messaging systems often involve multiple services, open interfaces, and cross-region communication—all of which introduce potential vulnerabilities if not addressed carefully. This section outlines comprehensive security best practices across Azure messaging services—Service Bus, Event Grid, Event Hubs, and Storage Queues—and provides implementation guidance for authentication, authorization, network isolation, encryption, auditing, and compliance.

1. Identity and Access Management

Properly securing access to messaging services starts with robust **authentication and authorization** mechanisms.

Azure Active Directory (Azure AD)

Use **Azure AD-based access control** wherever supported. This enables granular permissions using **role-based access control (RBAC)** and integrates with enterprise identity systems.

Example: Assigning the Azure Service Bus Data Sender role to an application principal.

```
az role assignment create \

—assignee "<client-id>" \
```

—role "Azure Service Bus Data Sender" \

—scope "/subscriptions/<sub-id>/resourceGroups/<rg>/providers/Microsoft.ServiceBus/namespaces/<namespace>"

Benefits:

- Centralized identity management
- Supports conditional access policies
- Reduces key sprawl and rotation complexity

Shared Access Signatures (SAS)

For legacy or non-AAD scenarios, services like Service Bus and Storage Queues support **SAS tokens**. While convenient, SAS tokens must be protected diligently.

Best practices:

- Use short-lived SAS tokens
- Assign least privilege (e.g., Send, Listen, not Manage)
- Store SAS tokens securely (e.g., in **Azure Key Vault**)

az storage queue generate-sas \

—account-name mystorage \

—name myqueue \

—permissions ra \

—expiry 2025-12-31T23:59Z \

—output tsv

2. Network Security

Securing network access is essential to reduce the attack surface of your real-time systems.

Private Endpoints

Where supported (e.g., Event Hubs, Service Bus Premium, Storage), use **private endpoints** to restrict traffic to your Azure Virtual Network (VNet).

resource privateEndpoint 'Microsoft.Network/privateEndpoints@2021-05-01' = {

name: 'eventhub-private-endpoint'

location: 'eastus'

properties: {

subnet: {

id: subnet.id

}

privateLinkServiceConnections: [

{

name: 'eventhub-connection'

properties: {

```
privateLinkServiceId: eventHubNamespace.id
groupIds: ['namespace']
}
}
]
}
}
```

Benefits:

- Ensures traffic never traverses public internet
- Prevents data exfiltration attacks
- Supports VNet Service Endpoints and NSG filtering

IP Filtering and Firewall Rules

If private endpoints are not available, restrict access using **IP firewall rules** to allow only trusted ranges.

- Enable **default deny** policies
- Use **Azure Front Door** or **Application Gateway** for controlled ingress

3. Data Encryption

Encryption In Transit

All Azure messaging services use **TLS 1.2** or higher for data in transit. No manual action is required, but ensure your clients also enforce strong protocols.

- Disable legacy protocols (e.g., TLS 1.0, 1.1)
- Validate certificates where custom clients are used

Encryption At Rest

Azure automatically encrypts data at rest using **Microsoft-managed keys**. For additional control:

- Use **Customer-Managed Keys (CMKs)** stored in Azure Key Vault
- Enable **key rotation policies**

Example Bicep snippet:

```
resource keyVault 'Microsoft.KeyVault/vaults@2021-10-01' = { ... }

resource key 'Microsoft.KeyVault/vaults/keys@2021-10-01' = {

name: '${keyVault.name}/servicebus-key'

properties: {

keySize: 2048

kty: 'RSA'
```

```
}
}
resource sbNamespace 'Microsoft.ServiceBus/namespaces@2022-10-01-preview' = {
name: 'secure-servicebus'
location: 'eastus'
properties: {
encryption: {
keySource: 'Microsoft.KeyVault'
keyVaultProperties: [
{
keyName: 'servicebus-key'
keyVaultUri: keyVault.properties.vaultUri
}
]
}
}
}
```

4. Message Validation and Sanitization

To prevent injection attacks or malformed data processing:

- Use strict **schema validation** (e.g., JSON schema for events)
- Sanitize all input fields before processing
- Reject messages that fail validation at the earliest point

With Event Grid and Event Hubs, implement validation in your consumer applications or use schema registries where applicable.

5. Least Privilege Principle

Apply the **least privilege** principle at every level:

- Use RBAC to assign minimal permissions to identities
- Avoid reusing credentials across services
- Isolate production, staging, and development environments

Create **separate namespaces** and **service principals** for each environment and function to prevent cross-contamination.

6. Monitoring, Auditing, and Threat Detection

Visibility into system activity is essential for detecting anomalies and responding to incidents.

Diagnostic Settings

Enable **diagnostic logging** for all messaging services. Route logs to:

- **Azure Monitor Logs** for query and alerting

- **Storage Account** for archival
- **Event Hub** for centralized log streaming

Example:

```
az monitor diagnostic-settings create \
—resource <eventhub-id> \
—name 'eh-logs' \
—logs '[{"category":"OperationalLogs","enabled":true}]' \
—workspace <log-analytics-id>
```

Activity Logs

Use **Azure Activity Logs** to track configuration changes, authentication attempts, and network access.

Azure Defender for Cloud

Enable Azure Defender to detect anomalies such as:

- Unusual data volume
- Unauthorized access attempts
- Usage from unexpected geographies

Use **Security Center recommendations** to remediate weak configurations.

7. Handling Sensitive Data

Avoid placing sensitive data (e.g., PII, secrets) directly in messages or events. Instead:

- Store sensitive payloads in **Key Vault** or **secure storage**
- Include only secure references (e.g., URI + token)
- Enforce access controls on the referenced resource

Ensure compliance with standards like **GDPR**, **HIPAA**, or **PCI-DSS** depending on data classification.

8. Secure Development Practices

Enforce security during development:

- Use **DevSecOps** with CI/CD pipelines
- Run **static analysis tools** (e.g., Microsoft Security DevOps)
- Use **code scanning** for credential leaks
- Automate infrastructure with **ARM/Bicep/Terraform** to maintain consistency and review changes

Example: GitHub Actions pipeline with secret scanning and security linting.

```
- name: Run Security Scan

uses: microsoft/security-devops-action@latest
```

9. Denial of Service (DoS) Mitigation

Messaging systems can be targeted by flooding attacks or misconfigured services:

- Set **rate limits** in consuming functions and APIs
- Use **Service Bus MaxDeliveryCount** and **lock duration** to throttle retries
- Apply **event filtering** in Event Grid to reduce unnecessary delivery
- Use **Azure API Management** or **App Gateway WAF** to shield public endpoints

10. Secure Cross-Service Integration

When integrating messaging with other services:

- Use **Managed Identity** for authentication
- Define **service-to-service policies** using **Azure Policy**
- Audit **access tokens** and permissions periodically

Example: Allow only a specific Function App to write to a Service Bus topic.

```
resource assignment 'Microsoft.Authorization/roleAssignments@2020-04-01-preview' = {

name: guid(functionApp.id, sbNamespace.id, 'data-sender-role')

properties: {
```

```
roleDefinitionId:
subscriptionResourceId('Microsoft.Authorization/roleDefinitions',
'Send Role ID')

principalId: functionApp.identity.principalId

scope: sbNamespace.id

}

}
```

Summary

Securing real-time messaging solutions in Azure requires a defense-in-depth approach that combines identity management, network controls, encryption, monitoring, and operational discipline. By following best practices across each layer of your architecture—data, code, infrastructure, and policy—you can ensure that your messaging flows are protected against both accidental misconfiguration and deliberate attack.

With capabilities such as private networking, managed identities, diagnostic logging, encryption with customer-managed keys, and centralized monitoring, Azure equips developers and architects to meet even the most demanding security and compliance requirements. In the chapters ahead, we will explore practical implementations and operational strategies for deploying, monitoring, and evolving secure and scalable real-time applications in the Azure ecosystem.

Chapter 5: Implementing Azure Service Bus

Setting Up Topics and Queues

Azure Service Bus provides enterprise-grade message brokering capabilities, including support for both queue-based point-to-point communication and topic-based publish-subscribe patterns. Properly setting up Service Bus queues and topics is essential for building scalable, reliable, and maintainable messaging architectures. This section focuses on the setup, configuration, and best practices for implementing queues and topics within Service Bus using the Azure Portal, Azure CLI, Bicep, and SDKs.

Overview of Queues vs. Topics

- **Queues** provide point-to-point messaging. A single consumer receives each message.
- **Topics** support a publish-subscribe model, allowing multiple subscribers to receive copies of each message published to a topic.

When to use:

- Use **queues** for load distribution and task queuing.
- Use **topics** when multiple consumers need to react to the same message (e.g., logging, analytics, notification).

Creating a Service Bus Namespace

A **namespace** is a container for all messaging components, including queues and topics. It represents a fully qualified domain under which Service Bus entities operate.

Using Azure Portal

1. Navigate to *Service Bus > Create.*
2. Choose a name (e.g., my-messaging-namespace).
3. Select the pricing tier:
   - **Basic**: Queues only
   - **Standard**: Queues and topics
   - **Premium**: Dedicated resources, better performance, VNet support
4. Choose the region and redundancy settings.
5. Review and create.

Using Azure CLI

```
az servicebus namespace create \
—name myNamespace \
—resource-group myResourceGroup \
—location eastus \
—sku Premium
```

Creating a Queue

Queues are used for decoupled communication between producers and a single consumer.

Key Properties:

- **MaxDeliveryCount**: Number of delivery attempts before dead-lettering
- **LockDuration**: Duration a message is locked for processing
- **MessageTTL**: Expiry for undelivered messages
- **Partitioning**: Enable for scalability
- **Duplicate Detection**: Prevent message re-processing

Azure CLI Example

az servicebus queue create \

—resource-group myResourceGroup \

—namespace-name myNamespace \

—name order-queue \

—enable-duplicate-detection true \

—duplicate-detection-history-time-window PT10M \

—max-delivery-count 10 \

—lock-duration PT5M \

—enable-dead-lettering-on-message-expiration true

Bicep Definition

resource sbNamespace 'Microsoft.ServiceBus/namespaces@2022-10-01-preview' = {

name: 'orders-namespace'

location: 'eastus'

sku: {

name: 'Premium'

tier: 'Premium'

}

}

resource orderQueue 'Microsoft.ServiceBus/namespaces/queues@2022-10-01-preview' = {

name: '${sbNamespace.name}/order-queue'

properties: {

lockDuration: 'PT5M'

maxDeliveryCount: 10

enablePartitioning: true

requiresDuplicateDetection: true

duplicateDetectionHistoryTimeWindow: 'PT10M'

```
}
}
```

Creating a Topic and Subscriptions

Topics allow messages to be broadcasted to multiple **subscriptions**, each functioning as a virtual queue.

Use Case Example:

An e-commerce system publishes an OrderCreated message:

- Billing service subscribes and charges the customer.
- Inventory system reserves the items.
- Notification system emails the user.

Azure CLI Example

```
az servicebus topic create \
—resource-group myResourceGroup \
—namespace-name myNamespace \
—name order-topic
az servicebus topic subscription create \
—resource-group myResourceGroup \
—namespace-name myNamespace \
—topic-name order-topic \
```

—name billing-subscription

az servicebus topic subscription create \

—resource-group myResourceGroup \

—namespace-name myNamespace \

—topic-name order-topic \

—name inventory-subscription

Adding a SQL Filter to a Subscription

You can filter messages at the subscription level to deliver only those that match certain criteria.

az servicebus topic subscription rule create \

—resource-group myResourceGroup \

—namespace-name myNamespace \

—topic-name order-topic \

—subscription-name billing-subscription \

—name only-high-value \

—filter-sql-expression "totalAmount > 1000"

Sending and Receiving Messages

Sending to a Queue

var client = new ServiceBusClient(connectionString);

```
var sender = client.CreateSender("order-queue");

await sender.SendMessageAsync(new ServiceBusMessage("Order ID: 12345"));
```

Receiving from a Queue

```
var receiver = client.CreateReceiver("order-queue");

ServiceBusReceivedMessage message = await receiver.ReceiveMessageAsync();

Console.WriteLine(message.Body.ToString());

await receiver.CompleteMessageAsync(message);
```

Working with Sessions

Enable **sessions** to guarantee FIFO delivery within a message group (e.g., per customer, per order).

```
az servicebus queue create \

—resource-group myResourceGroup \

—namespace-name myNamespace \

—name session-enabled-queue \

—enable-session true
```

In code, receive using AcceptNextSessionAsync() or specify session ID.

```
var sessionReceiver = await client.AcceptNextSessionAsync("session-enabled-queue");
```

```
ServiceBusReceivedMessage sessionMessage = await sessionReceiver.ReceiveMessageAsync();
```

Retry and Dead-Letter Settings

Messages that can't be processed successfully after MaxDeliveryCount attempts are sent to a **dead-letter queue (DLQ)**.

DLQ Characteristics:

- Auto-created for every queue or subscription.
- Path: <entity>/Subscriptions/<name>/$DeadLetterQueue
- Use it to inspect and reprocess failed messages.

```
var dlqReceiver = client.CreateReceiver("order-queue", new ServiceBusReceiverOptions {

SubQueue = SubQueue.DeadLetter

});
```

Monitoring and Diagnostics

Enable **diagnostic settings** to track metrics and logs.

```
az monitor diagnostic-settings create \

—name sb-monitoring \

—resource /subscriptions/<id>/resourceGroups/<rg>/providers/Microsoft.ServiceBus/namespaces/myNamespace \

—workspace <log-analytics-id> \
```

—logs '[{"category":"OperationalLogs","enabled":true}]'

Metrics include:

- ActiveMessages
- DeadLetteredMessages
- IncomingRequests
- SuccessfulRequests

Set up alerts for queue depth or message processing failures.

Best Practices

1. **Use Premium tier** for production workloads.
2. **Enable partitioning** for large queues/topics.
3. **Set lock duration** based on processing time.
4. **Use sessions** only when order is critical.
5. **Apply filters** to reduce load on subscriptions.
6. **Batch send/receive** messages for performance.
7. **Monitor dead-letter queues** proactively.
8. **Implement retry logic** with exponential backoff.
9. **Use message IDs** to support deduplication.
10. **Isolate environments** by using separate namespaces.

Summary

Setting up Azure Service Bus queues and topics correctly is the foundation of a reliable, scalable messaging infrastructure. Whether you're enabling simple asynchronous communication or building complex pub-sub workflows, understanding the configuration options, capabilities, and limitations of these entities ensures that your system is both performant and resilient.

Subsequent sections will explore message serialization, dead-letter handling, and integrating Service Bus with other Azure services like Functions, Logic Apps, and Event Grid to enable fully automated and decoupled real-time solutions.

Message Serialization and Deserialization

Serialization and deserialization are critical in the context of Azure Service Bus messaging. Serialization is the process of converting an object into a format suitable for transmission or storage—typically into JSON, XML, Avro, or binary. Deserialization is the reverse process: transforming the received message back into a usable object within the consuming application. Real-time systems require efficient, secure, and consistent message formats to support interoperability, reduce latency, and ensure message integrity across distributed services.

This section explores key strategies, considerations, and implementations for serializing and deserializing messages with Azure Service Bus, using various formats and programming languages, focusing especially on JSON, which is the de facto standard for service-based communication.

Why Serialization Matters

In Service Bus, messages must be represented as binary payloads—usually encoded into a byte stream within the message's Body. The metadata (such as ContentType and custom ApplicationProperties) can further assist in identifying how to handle the message.

Benefits of Proper Serialization

- **Interoperability**: Allows multiple systems with different technologies to process the same message.
- **Validation**: Schemas can be enforced to validate structure and types.
- **Performance**: Compact and efficient formats (e.g., binary, Avro) can reduce bandwidth.
- **Security**: Prevents malicious content through validation and control.

Common Formats

JSON

- Human-readable
- Widely supported
- Ideal for integration with web apps, mobile clients, and Azure Functions

XML

- Verbose but mature
- Schema-rich with strong validation via XSD
- Suitable for legacy enterprise systems

Binary / Avro / Protobuf

- Compact, efficient
- Requires schema registration and careful versioning
- Preferred for high-throughput telemetry (e.g., IoT)

Setting ContentType

The ContentType property on a Service Bus message helps consumers identify the format.

```
var message = new ServiceBusMessage(Encoding.UTF8.GetBytes(jsonPayload))

{

ContentType = "application/json",

Subject = "UserRegistered"

};
```

Consumers should inspect ContentType before parsing the message.

Serializing Objects

JSON (C# Example)

```
var user = new User {

Id = "U001",

Name = "Alice",
```

```
Email = "alice@example.com"

};

string json = JsonSerializer.Serialize(user);

var message = new ServiceBusMessage(Encoding.UTF8.GetBytes(json))

{

ContentType = "application/json",

Subject = "UserCreated",

ApplicationProperties = {

["eventType"] = "UserCreated"

}

};
```

The payload is serialized to UTF-8 encoded JSON. Always validate or sanitize data before sending.

XML (C# Example)

```
var serializer = new XmlSerializer(typeof(User));

using var ms = new MemoryStream();

serializer.Serialize(ms, user);

var message = new ServiceBusMessage(ms.ToArray())

{
```

```
ContentType = "application/xml"

};
```

Make sure your consumers can parse and handle XML payloads securely, avoiding XML External Entity (XXE) vulnerabilities.

Deserializing Messages

Consumers should use the ContentType or ApplicationProperties["eventType"] to determine how to deserialize the message body.

JSON (C# Consumer)

```
ServiceBusReceivedMessage message = await receiver.ReceiveMessageAsync();

string json = Encoding.UTF8.GetString(message.Body);

var user = JsonSerializer.Deserialize<User>(json);
```

JSON (Node.js Consumer)

```
const message = await receiver.receiveMessages(1);

const payload = JSON.parse(message.body.toString('utf8'));

console.log(payload.name);
```

Ensure proper error handling for unexpected formats or corrupted payloads.

Schema Evolution and Versioning

Message schemas must evolve without breaking existing consumers. Strategies include:

- **Versioned Event Types**: Use event type names like UserCreated.v1 or include a dataVersion field.
- **Optional Fields**: Add new fields that do not affect existing consumers.
- **Backward-Compatible Changes**: Avoid deleting fields or changing their types.

```
{
"eventType": "UserCreated",
"dataVersion": "1.0",
"data": {
"userId": "U001",
"name": "Alice",
"email": "alice@example.com",
"createdAt": "2025-05-09T12:00:00Z"
}
}
```

Consumers should ignore unknown fields to support forward compatibility.

Validating Message Content

Before processing, validate message structure and data types. Use tools like:

- **System.Text.Json with JsonSchema.Net**
- **FluentValidation**
- **Custom schema validation logic**

Example: JSON schema validation in .NET

```
var schema = JsonSchema.FromText(jsonSchemaText);

var errors = schema.Validate(jsonString);

if (errors.Any()) throw new InvalidDataException("Invalid payload");
```

For XML, use XSD-based validation.

Compressing Messages

For large payloads:

- Compress message body using GZip or Deflate
- Set ContentEncoding property accordingly

```
byte[] compressed = CompressGzip(Encoding.UTF8.GetBytes(json));

var message = new ServiceBusMessage(compressed)

{
```

ContentType = "application/json",

ContentEncoding = "gzip"

};

Ensure the receiver decompresses before deserialization.

Enriching Messages with Metadata

Use **ApplicationProperties** to add routing or context information without altering the payload.

message.ApplicationProperties["tenantId"] = "T001";

message.ApplicationProperties["priority"] = "high";

This helps with filtering in topics or diagnostic correlation.

Securing Serialized Messages

Serialization can introduce vulnerabilities if misused:

- **Do not trust serialized input blindly**
- **Avoid using BinaryFormatter** or insecure deserializers
- **Use allowlists** of types when deserializing
- **Limit maximum payload size**

Always enforce authentication and authorization before processing the message.

Handling Failures and Dead-Lettering

Invalid messages should be **dead-lettered** for inspection rather than causing consumer crashes.

```
await receiver.DeadLetterMessageAsync(message, "ValidationError",
"Invalid format");
```

Regularly monitor and analyze dead-letter queues to update deserialization logic and improve schema validation.

Testing and Observability

Include serialization tests in your CI pipelines:

- Unit test each event type
- Validate against JSON schema
- Verify round-trip serialization/deserialization

Add tracing and telemetry to record eventType, ContentType, message size, and processing time.

```
logger.LogInformation("Received event {EventType}, Size: {Size}",
message.ApplicationProperties["eventType"],
message.Body.Length);
```

Summary

Message serialization and deserialization are foundational to robust messaging with Azure Service Bus. They determine how effectively your services can communicate, scale, and evolve. By choosing the right serialization format, enforcing schema validation, planning for versioning, and handling errors gracefully, you ensure that your real-time system remains reliable, performant, and future-proof.

In the next section, we will address the mechanics of dead-letter messages—how they are created, monitored, and processed, and how to design resilient systems that respond gracefully to failures in message handling.

Handling Dead-Letter Messages

In any real-time messaging system, not all messages can or should be processed successfully. Failures may occur due to malformed data, system outages, logic errors, security violations, or even business rule violations. Azure Service Bus provides a built-in mechanism called the **Dead-Letter Queue (DLQ)** to safely handle such unprocessable messages without losing them. This allows developers and operators to inspect, diagnose, and reprocess or discard problematic messages while maintaining the integrity of the primary message flow.

This section focuses on the principles, configurations, diagnostics, and recovery strategies for managing dead-letter messages in Azure Service Bus queues and topic subscriptions.

What is a Dead-Letter Queue?

A **Dead-Letter Queue** is a sub-queue that stores messages that cannot be delivered to a receiver or processed successfully. Every queue and subscription in Azure Service Bus automatically supports a DLQ without needing to create a separate resource.

DLQ Characteristics:

- It has the same message structure as the original queue.
- It is accessible via a special path: <entity-path>/$DeadLetterQueue.

- Messages in DLQ can be retrieved, examined, fixed, and optionally returned to the main queue.

Common Reasons for Dead-Lettering

1. **Exceeded Maximum Delivery Count**: The message was delivered more times than allowed and was not completed.
2. **Time to Live (TTL) Expired**: The message was not processed within its TTL and expired.
3. **Explicit Dead-Lettering by Consumer**: Consumer code chose to dead-letter due to custom business logic.
4. **Filter Evaluation Exceptions**: Message could not be evaluated against a subscription filter.
5. **Deserialization or Validation Failure**: Receiver could not parse or validate the message content.

Configuring Dead-Lettering

You can configure dead-lettering during queue or subscription creation.

Example using Azure CLI:

az servicebus queue create \

—resource-group myRG \

—namespace-name myNamespace \

—name orders-queue \

—enable-dead-lettering-on-message-expiration true \

—max-delivery-count 5

Example using Bicep:

```
resource ordersQueue 'Microsoft.ServiceBus/namespaces/queues@2022-10-01-preview' = {

name: 'orders-queue'

parent: sbNamespace

properties: {

maxDeliveryCount: 5

enableDeadLetteringOnMessageExpiration: true

}

}
```

Sending Messages to DLQ from Consumer Code

Messages can be explicitly dead-lettered by receivers for known failures.

Example in C#:

```
try

{

var message = await receiver.ReceiveMessageAsync();

var order = JsonSerializer.Deserialize<Order>(message.Body);

if (!IsValid(order))
```

```
{
await receiver.DeadLetterMessageAsync(message, "ValidationError", "Order is invalid.");
return;
}
await ProcessOrderAsync(order);
await receiver.CompleteMessageAsync(message);
}
catch (Exception ex)
{
logger.LogError(ex, "Unhandled exception");
// Do not complete message – it will be retried
}
```

Parameters for DeadLetterMessageAsync include:

- reason: A short string describing the problem
- errorDescription: A more detailed message
- These are stored in the dead-lettered message's metadata

Reading from the Dead-Letter Queue

To retrieve messages from a DLQ, specify the **SubQueue.DeadLetter** option when creating a receiver.

Example in C#:

```
var receiver = client.CreateReceiver("orders-queue", new ServiceBusReceiverOptions {

SubQueue = SubQueue.DeadLetter

});

ServiceBusReceivedMessage dlqMessage = await receiver.ReceiveMessageAsync();

Console.WriteLine(dlqMessage.DeadLetterReason);

Console.WriteLine(dlqMessage.DeadLetterErrorDescription);

Console.WriteLine(Encoding.UTF8.GetString(dlqMessage.Body));
```

For topic subscriptions:

```
var receiver = client.CreateReceiver("orders-topic", "billing-subscription", new ServiceBusReceiverOptions {

SubQueue = SubQueue.DeadLetter

});
```

Monitoring DLQ Usage

Azure Monitor exposes DLQ metrics to observe and alert on system health.

Key Metrics:

- DeadLetteredMessages
- Messages

- TransferDeadLetteredMessages

Use **Log Analytics** or **Grafana** to plot DLQ growth trends and trigger alerts when thresholds are exceeded.

Azure CLI Example for Alerts:

```
az monitor metrics alert create \
—name "DLQOverflowAlert" \
—resource "/subscriptions/.../serviceBus/namespaces/myNamespace/queues/orders-queue" \
—condition "total DeadLetteredMessages > 100" \
—description "Too many messages in DLQ"
```

Diagnosing DLQ Issues

When analyzing messages in DLQ, investigate:

- **DeadLetterReason**: Indicates why the message was sent to DLQ.
- **DeadLetterErrorDescription**: Additional human-readable message.
- **ApplicationProperties**: Custom context passed with the message.
- **Body Content**: Check for malformed payloads or schema mismatches.

Common scenarios:

- MaxDeliveryCountExceeded: Consumer might not be acknowledging messages due to crash or unhandled exception.

- TimeToLiveExpired: Downstream system might be unavailable or too slow.

- Custom ValidationError: Consumer logic rejected the payload.

Reprocessing Messages from DLQ

Messages in the DLQ are not automatically reprocessed. You can reprocess them manually or through automation:

Option 1: Manual Review

Download messages via Azure Portal or Service Bus Explorer to examine, fix, and requeue them.

Option 2: Programmatic Requeue

Use an Azure Function, Logic App, or worker to move messages from DLQ to the main queue.

```
var message = await dlqReceiver.ReceiveMessageAsync();

var requeuedMessage = new ServiceBusMessage(message.Body)

{

ContentType = message.ContentType,

Subject = message.Subject,
```

```
ApplicationProperties = message.ApplicationProperties
};
await mainQueueSender.SendMessageAsync(requeuedMessage);
await dlqReceiver.CompleteMessageAsync(message);
```

Ensure that problematic data or logic has been resolved before requeueing.

Automating DLQ Processing with Azure Functions

Use Azure Functions with **ServiceBusTrigger** and queueName/$DeadLetterQueue to automate DLQ inspections.

```
[FunctionName("DeadLetterProcessor")]
public async Task Run(
[ServiceBusTrigger("orders-queue/$DeadLetterQueue", Connection = "ServiceBusConnection")]
ServiceBusReceivedMessage message,
ILogger log)
{
log.LogWarning("Dead-lettered message received: {Reason} - {Description}",
message.DeadLetterReason, message.DeadLetterErrorDescription);
// Route to error handler or trigger reprocessing
}
```

You can also forward DLQ content to another queue for deferred processing.

Best Practices

1. **Always configure MaxDeliveryCount** and TTL appropriately.
2. **Use explicit dead-lettering** when business logic fails (e.g., fraud detection, validation).
3. **Instrument consumer logs** with message diagnostics and correlation IDs.
4. **Monitor DLQs** actively and alert on growth trends.
5. **Automate cleanup or requeueing** with retry policies and poison message handling.
6. **Inspect message metadata** to identify root causes and patterns.
7. **Document known DLQ reasons** and standardize error codes across teams.

DLQ vs Transfer DLQ

Azure Service Bus also supports **Transfer Dead-Letter Queues:**

- Messages forwarded between entities that fail to be delivered land here.
- Path: entity/$Transfer/$DeadLetterQueue

Use this for chained messaging topologies where intermediate failures may occur.

Summary

Dead-letter queues are an essential safeguard in Azure Service Bus that ensure no message is lost even when processing fails. By understanding how and why messages are dead-lettered, setting appropriate thresholds, monitoring with alerts, and building robust recovery workflows, you can maintain system resilience, detect data issues early, and minimize downtime in real-time applications.

The next section explores how to integrate Service Bus with other Azure services—such as Azure Functions, Logic Apps, Event Grid, and more—to create end-to-end automation and orchestrated workflows using messages as triggers across the Azure ecosystem.

Integrating with Other Azure Services

Azure Service Bus is rarely used in isolation. Its true power emerges when it acts as the backbone of distributed applications, seamlessly integrating with various Azure services such as Azure Functions, Logic Apps, Azure Event Grid, Azure API Management, Azure Synapse, and monitoring solutions like Azure Monitor and Application Insights. This integration capability allows developers to create scalable, resilient, and loosely coupled systems that can react to events, orchestrate workflows, handle failures gracefully, and expose services securely.

This section explores how Azure Service Bus integrates with the broader Azure ecosystem. We'll examine service-to-service workflows, serverless messaging architectures, orchestration and event routing, observability, and secure front-door patterns.

Integrating with Azure Functions

Azure Functions provides a serverless compute platform that automatically scales based on the volume of messages. It supports **Service Bus triggers**, allowing you to build event-driven workflows and processing logic without managing infrastructure.

Queue Trigger Example

```
[FunctionName("ProcessOrder")]

public static async Task Run(

[ServiceBusTrigger("order-queue", Connection = "ServiceBusConnection")] string message,

ILogger log)

{

log.LogInformation($"Order received: {message}");

// Business logic

}
```

Key features:

- Supports both **queues** and **topic subscriptions**
- Automatically handles message retries
- Scales horizontally with message volume
- Compatible with **session-enabled** entities

Configuration

Set up the ServiceBusConnection in local.settings.json:

```
{
"Values": {
"AzureWebJobsStorage": "...",
"ServiceBusConnection":
"Endpoint=sb://myservicebus.servicebus.windows.net/;SharedAccessKey
}
}
```

Use the **Premium Plan** or **Elastic Premium** tier to avoid cold start issues in latency-sensitive applications.

Integrating with Logic Apps

Azure Logic Apps provides a low-code/no-code platform for creating automated workflows using connectors. It natively supports Service Bus as a trigger and action, making it ideal for integrating messaging into business processes.

Trigger Example: New Message in Queue

1. Trigger: When a message is received in order-queue
2. Condition: If priority = high
3. Action: Send an email via Outlook connector

Use Cases:

- Notify teams of important events

- Automatically escalate errors
- Connect to CRM or ERP systems

Logic Apps also supports **peek-lock semantics** and **dead-letter handling.**

Example Workflow Actions

- Trigger: Service Bus (receive message)
- Action: SQL Server (insert order record)
- Action: Outlook (send order notification)

Logic Apps can be used as glue logic to orchestrate across Azure, SaaS, and on-premises systems.

Using Azure Event Grid for Event Routing

While Service Bus handles message queuing and processing, **Azure Event Grid** is designed for lightweight, reactive event routing. Integrating Service Bus with Event Grid allows for event-driven architectures where events trigger messages into queues or topics for processing.

Integration Pattern

1. An Event Grid subscription is configured to forward specific events to a Service Bus topic.
2. Subscribers to the topic (e.g., Azure Functions, Logic Apps) handle the event.

```
resource eventSubscription 'Microsoft.EventGrid/eventSubscriptions@2022-06-15' = {
name: 'BlobCreatedToServiceBus'
scope: storageAccount
properties: {
destination: {
endpointType: 'ServiceBusTopic'
properties: {
resourceId: topic.id
}
}
filter: {
includedEventTypes: ['Microsoft.Storage.BlobCreated']
}
}
}
```

This integration is useful for connecting storage events, resource lifecycle events, or custom business events with downstream message handlers.

Connecting with Azure API Management

Azure API Management (APIM) provides a secure and controlled gateway to expose Service Bus-backed APIs. You can expose endpoints that enqueue messages to Service Bus, effectively decoupling client requests from backend processing.

Scenario: API for Submitting Orders

- Client sends HTTP request to /submitOrder
- APIM validates and logs the request
- Backend API handler enqueues message to order-queue
- Azure Function processes the order asynchronously

This pattern improves:

- **Responsiveness**: Client doesn't wait for processing to complete
- **Resilience**: Failures are isolated and retryable
- **Security**: APIM handles authentication, rate limiting, and request validation

Example Policy Snippet

```
<send-request mode="new" response-variable-name="response">

<set-url>https://myfunction.azurewebsites.net/api/EnqueueOrder</set-url>

<set-method>POST</set-method>
```

```
<set-body>@(context.Request.Body.As<string>())</set-body>

</send-request>
```

Use **Managed Identity** to authenticate securely without embedding secrets.

Data Integration with Azure Synapse and Data Factory

Service Bus is frequently used to trigger data pipelines or signal the availability of new data.

Patterns

- A message in data-queue triggers an Azure Function that starts a **Synapse Pipeline** via REST.
- **Azure Data Factory** monitors a Service Bus queue for orchestration signals using **Webhook Activity**.

Use Case

When a data export job completes, a message is placed on export-notifications. This triggers downstream pipelines to copy data, apply transformations, or send audit logs.

Observability with Azure Monitor and Application Insights

Integration is not complete without **visibility** into what your system is doing.

Key Metrics to Monitor

- IncomingRequests
- ThrottledRequests
- ActiveMessages
- DeadLetteredMessages

Example Alert

```
az monitor metrics alert create \

—name "DLQThreshold" \

—resource "/subscriptions/xxx/serviceBus/namespaces/ns/queues/queue" \

—condition "total DeadLetteredMessages > 100" \

—description "High dead-letter message count"
```

Use **Application Insights** SDK to track custom events:

```
telemetryClient.TrackEvent("MessageEnqueued", new Dictionary<string, string> {

["queue"] = "order-queue",

["messageId"] = message.MessageId

});
```

Secure Service-to-Service Communication

When services exchange messages over Service Bus, secure authentication and authorization are critical.

Managed Identity

Use **Managed Identities** for VMs, Functions, and App Services to authenticate to Service Bus without credentials.

```
resource identity 'Microsoft.ManagedIdentity/userAssignedIdentities@2022-01-31-preview' = {

name: 'functionIdentity'

}

resource roleAssignment 'Microsoft.Authorization/roleAssignments@2022-04-01' = {

name: guid(identity.id, 'Azure Service Bus Data Sender')

properties: {

principalId: identity.properties.principalId

roleDefinitionId: '/providers/Microsoft.Authorization/roleDefinitions/role-id'

scope: sbNamespace.id

}

}
```

Assign roles like:

- Azure Service Bus Data Sender
- Azure Service Bus Data Receiver

This avoids hardcoded credentials and supports fine-grained access control.

Hybrid and Edge Integration

For scenarios requiring communication with on-premises or edge devices:

- Use **Azure IoT Hub** to ingest messages and route to Service Bus for downstream processing.
- Use **VPN or ExpressRoute** to securely integrate on-prem applications with Service Bus via VNet.

Summary

Azure Service Bus is a versatile integration layer that supports deep, seamless connectivity across Azure services and external systems. Whether you're orchestrating workflows with Logic Apps, triggering Functions on message arrival, routing events via Event Grid, or exposing queue-backed APIs through APIM, Service Bus plays a central role in modern cloud architectures.

By using built-in connectors, SDKs, managed identities, and monitoring integrations, developers can build secure, scalable, and resilient solutions without reinventing infrastructure. The next chapter will shift focus from Service Bus to mastering Azure Event Grid, exploring its publish-subscribe model, advanced filtering, custom domains, and security integrations.

Chapter 6: Mastering Azure Event Grid

Event Publishing and Subscription Models

Azure Event Grid is a highly scalable, fully managed event routing service that enables reactive, event-driven architectures in the cloud. It decouples event producers from event consumers, allowing each to evolve independently. Event Grid supports multiple publishing models and subscription mechanisms that are foundational to building real-time, loosely coupled systems. This section dives deep into how events are published to Event Grid and how various Azure and custom services subscribe to and process these events.

Event-Driven Architecture in Azure

Before discussing the models, it's important to understand the Event Grid architecture, which includes the following components:

- **Event Sources**: The originators of events, such as Blob Storage, Event Hubs, or custom apps.
- **Event Topics**: Channels where events are published.
- **Event Subscriptions**: Rules that route events from a topic to an event handler.
- **Event Handlers**: Services or endpoints that react to the event (e.g., Azure Functions, Logic Apps).

Event Publishing Models

1. System Topics (Built-In Sources)

System topics are automatically created and managed by Azure when subscribing to events from Azure services like:

- Azure Storage
- Azure Event Hubs
- Azure Container Registry
- Azure Key Vault
- Azure Media Services
- Azure App Configuration

These topics are scoped to a specific Azure resource and do not require manual provisioning.

```
az eventgrid event-subscription create \

—name blob-created-sub \

—source-resource-id
/subscriptions/<sub>/resourceGroups/<rg>/providers/
Microsoft.Storage/storageAccounts/<account> \

—endpoint https://myfunction.azurewebsites.net/runtime/
webhooks/EventGrid?code=<function-key>
```

Use case: Automatically trigger a Function when a new blob is created.

2. Custom Topics (User-Defined)

Custom topics are manually created and used when building applications that emit business-specific events.

```
az eventgrid topic create \
—name orders-topic \
—resource-group myRG \
—location westus2
```

Once the topic is created, applications can publish events using HTTPS POST requests or SDKs.

```
POST https://orders-topic.<region>-1.eventgrid.azure.net/api/events
aeg-sas-key: <your-topic-key>
Content-Type: application/json
[
{
"id": "abc123",
"eventType": "OrderPlaced",
"subject": "/orders/123",
"data": {
"orderId": "123",
"total": 299.99
```

},

"eventTime": "2025-05-09T10:00:00Z",

"dataVersion": "1.0"

}

]

3. Event Domains (Multi-Tenant Scenarios)

Event Domains provide a scalable, namespace-based model for managing events across multiple tenants or services. They are built on top of Custom Topics and allow the separation of event publishers and subscribers using domain topics.

Use Case: SaaS providers hosting services for many clients can use domains to route events per customer.

```
az eventgrid domain create \

—name ecommerce-domain \

—resource-group myRG \

—location eastus
```

Each publisher sends events to a domain topic like /ecommerce-domain/tenants/retailer1/orders.

Subscription Models

An **Event Subscription** defines:

- Which events to listen for

- Where to send them
- Optional filters for fine-grained routing

Supported Destinations:

- Azure Functions
- Logic Apps
- Event Hubs
- Webhooks
- Storage Queues
- Hybrid Connections

1. Subscribing to System Topics

```
az eventgrid event-subscription create \

—name blob-created-sub \

—source-resource-id
/subscriptions/<sub>/resourceGroups/<rg>/providers/
Microsoft.Storage/storageAccounts/myStorage \

—endpoint-type azurefunction \

—endpoint
/subscriptions/<sub>/resourceGroups/<rg>/providers/
Microsoft.Web/sites/myfunction/functions/HandleBlob
```

2. Subscribing to Custom Topics

az eventgrid event-subscription create \

—name order-handler \

—source-resource-id /subscriptions/<sub>/resourceGroups/<rg>/providers/Microsoft.EventGrid/topics/orders-topic \

—endpoint https://myhandler.com/api/events

Use **SAS token**, **client cert**, or **AAD tokens** to secure custom webhook endpoints.

Filtering and Routing

Filters determine which events are delivered to a subscriber.

Event Type Filter

—included-event-types OrderPlaced OrderCancelled

Subject Filter

—subject-begins-with "/orders/" \

—subject-ends-with "/created"

Advanced Filtering

—advanced-filter data.total NumberGreaterThan 1000

This routes only high-value orders to the subscription.

Dead Lettering and Retry Policy

If an event cannot be delivered, Event Grid will retry with exponential backoff for up to 24 hours. If delivery continues to fail:

- Events can be **dead-lettered** into a Blob container for diagnostics.
- Subscribers can reprocess the dead-letter events manually.

—deadletter-destination blobstorage \

—storage-account myStorage \

—storage-container deadletter

Best Practices:

- Always validate event delivery success
- Use diagnostic settings for logging failures
- Monitor DLQ container periodically

Schema Types

Event Grid supports two schema formats:

1. **EventGrid Schema** (default)

{

"id": "123",

"eventType": "MyAppEvent",

"subject": "/app/resource",

"eventTime": "2025-05-09T12:00:00Z",

"dataVersion": "1.0",

"data": { ... }

}

1. **CloudEvents v1.0**

{

"specversion": "1.0",

"type": "com.example.order.created",

"source": "/orders",

"id": "abc-123",

"time": "2025-05-09T12:00:00Z",

"data": { ... }

}

Specify schema during topic or subscription creation.

Security Considerations

- **Authentication**: Use AAD or SAS tokens to publish securely.
- **Event Validation**: Event Grid sends a validation event for webhooks; your handler must echo back a validation code.

- **IP Restrictions**: Use firewall and VNet rules on endpoints.
- **Private Endpoints**: Supported in Premium tiers for secure routing.

Monitoring and Diagnostics

Enable diagnostics to track:

- Successful/failed event delivery
- Retry counts
- Latency

Route logs to:

- Log Analytics
- Event Hub (for SIEMs)
- Storage (for archival)

Practical Scenario

Use Case: A retail app needs to process orders and trigger downstream workflows.

1. **Event Producer**: E-commerce app posts OrderPlaced to a custom topic.
2. **Subscription 1**: Azure Function generates invoice.
3. **Subscription 2**: Logic App sends customer confirmation.
4. **Subscription 3**: Event Hub ingests data for real-time

analytics.

All components are decoupled, independently deployable, and resilient.

Summary

Azure Event Grid enables the seamless routing of events across Azure services and custom applications using powerful publish-subscribe patterns. By supporting system topics, custom topics, and domains, along with precise subscription filtering and robust delivery guarantees, Event Grid is a central component in modern serverless and event-driven designs. In the next section, we'll explore how to configure and leverage custom event domains for tenant isolation, scalability, and advanced architecture scenarios in multi-client environments.

Custom Event Domains

As event-driven architectures scale, especially in multi-tenant or microservices environments, managing numerous event publishers, topics, and subscriptions becomes increasingly complex. Azure Event Grid introduces **Event Domains** to address this need, providing a logical container for organizing event sources and subscriptions across tenants or business units. Custom Event Domains are ideal for SaaS platforms, decentralized systems, or any solution requiring isolation, scalability, and controlled access to events.

This section explores the design, creation, use cases, security, and operational best practices for leveraging Event Grid Custom Domains effectively in Azure.

What Is an Event Domain?

An **Event Domain** is a high-level abstraction in Event Grid designed to group multiple **domain topics** under a single namespace. Unlike standard custom topics, which are singular event sources, domains allow you to:

- Programmatically generate **topics per tenant, service, or team**
- Apply fine-grained **access control and routing**
- Manage events across a **multi-tenant landscape** with greater clarity

Each domain can contain thousands of **domain topics**, making it suitable for large-scale, event-based systems.

Domain vs Custom Topic

Feature	Custom Topic	Event Domain
Entity Type	Single event source	Container of domain topics
Use Case	Single app or bounded service	Multi-tenant or microservices platforms
Topics Managed	One per topic	Thousands per domain
Topic Naming	Static	Hierarchical and dynamic
Publisher Access	Single key/shared policy	Scoped to topic (tenant)
Subscription Routing	To individual topics	To domain topic or domain-wide
Scaling	Limited to topic limits	Horizontally scalable

When to Use Event Domains

1. Multi-Tenant SaaS Platforms

Each tenant (customer) gets a dedicated domain topic, ensuring isolation and access control.

2. Microservice-Based Architectures

Each service/component can be modeled as a domain topic, simplifying event publication and consumption.

3. Partner Ecosystems

Third-party developers or integrators can publish events to domain topics assigned to them without having full control over the entire system.

4. Large Internal Organizations

Departments, teams, or internal business units can publish and subscribe within isolated domains to ensure governance and scalability.

Creating an Event Domain

Azure CLI

az eventgrid domain create \

—name ecommerce-domain \

—resource-group myRG \

—location eastus \

—sku Basic

This creates a domain that can host multiple domain topics such as:

- /ecommerce-domain/orders
- /ecommerce-domain/returns
- /ecommerce-domain/inventory

Publishing Events to Domain Topics

Event publishers send events to a specific **domain topic** using the REST API or SDK.

Example: POST to Domain Topic

POST https://ecommerce-domain.eastus-1.eventgrid.azure.net/api/events/orders

aeg-sas-key: <key>

Content-Type: application/json

[

{

"id": "event-789",

"eventType": "InventoryUpdated",

"subject": "/items/sku-123",

```
"data": {
"sku": "sku-123",
"quantity": 150
},
"eventTime": "2025-05-09T14:32:00Z",
"dataVersion": "1.0"
}
]
```

The path /api/events/orders represents the domain topic within ecommerce-domain.

Subscribing to Domain Topics

Subscriptions can target:

- A **specific domain topic** (e.g., only /orders)
- **All topics** within the domain using * for wildcards

Create a subscription to a domain topic

```
az eventgrid domain event-subscription create \
—domain-name ecommerce-domain \
—name process-orders \
—resource-group myRG \
```

—endpoint https://myordersfunction.azurewebsites.net/runtime/webhooks/EventGrid?code=...

—included-event-types OrderPlaced OrderCancelled \

—subject-begins-with "/orders/"

Use advanced filters to route based on content fields, e.g. high-value orders only.

Domain-Wide Subscription

az eventgrid domain event-subscription create \

—domain-name ecommerce-domain \

—name process-all \

—resource-group myRG \

—endpoint https://analytics.azurewebsites.net/api/track

This captures all events across all domain topics.

Securing Event Domains

1. Topic-Level Authentication

You can assign **shared access keys** per domain topic, enabling scoped publisher access.

az eventgrid domain topic create \

—name returns \

—domain-name ecommerce-domain \

—resource-group myRG

2. Role-Based Access Control (RBAC)

Use **Azure RBAC** to manage who can publish to or subscribe from each domain topic.

Role Examples:

- EventGrid Event Publisher
- EventGrid Event Subscription Contributor

3. Private Endpoints

Use private endpoints (Premium SKU) to restrict network access and enforce VNet-only communication.

az network private-endpoint create \

—name myEndpoint \

—resource-group myRG \

—vnet-name myVNet \

—subnet mySubnet \

—private-connection-resource-id /subscriptions/xxx/resourceGroups/myRG/providers/Microsoft.EventGrid/domains/ecommerce-domain \

—group-id domain

Monitoring and Diagnostics

Enable **diagnostic logs** at the domain level to track event metrics, delivery failures, and subscriber performance.

```
az monitor diagnostic-settings create \

—name domain-logs \

—resource /subscriptions/<id>/resourceGroups/<rg>/providers/Microsoft.EventGrid/domains/ecommerce-domain \

—workspace <log-analytics-id> \

—logs '[{"category": "DeliveryFailures", "enabled": true}]'
```

Metrics include:

- PublishSuccessCount
- DeliveryFailedCount
- DeliveryThrottledCount

Configure **alerts** to notify operations when failures exceed thresholds.

Advanced Use Cases

1. Tenant Isolation

Each customer or tenant has a dedicated domain topic and secure publish credentials. Consumers can only subscribe to topics assigned to them.

2. Audit Logging

Publishers send both the primary event and an audit event to a secure internal domain topic for compliance and observability.

3. Multi-Region Replication

Use Event Grid domain topics with **Event Hubs** or **Azure Data Explorer** to stream and replicate events across regions for high availability.

4. Blue-Green Deployment

During phased rollouts, split traffic between multiple domain topics (e.g., /orders-v1, /orders-v2) to test new consumers.

Best Practices

- **Prefix domain topics with clear namespacing** (/tenants/123/orders)
- **Use wildcard subscriptions cautiously** to avoid unintended data exposure
- **Rotate SAS keys** and use AAD where possible
- **Minimize filtering at consumer side**—apply routing logic in subscriptions
- **Limit subscription fan-out** per topic to manage downstream load

---

Summary

Event Domains are a powerful abstraction for managing large-scale, multi-tenant, or complex event publishing scenarios in Azure. By organizing events into domain topics, applying secure boundaries, and leveraging advanced routing and filtering, architects gain fine control over how events are produced, consumed, and monitored.

In the next section, we'll focus on the routing and filtering capabilities within Event Grid subscriptions, showing how to create highly targeted event flows that reduce noise, improve processing efficiency, and enable rich real-time decision-making.

Advanced Routing and Filtering

Efficient event routing is the backbone of real-time cloud applications. In systems where hundreds or thousands of events are generated every second, it's critical to ensure that only relevant events are delivered to appropriate handlers. Azure Event Grid supports advanced routing and filtering capabilities that empower developers to define granular, high-performance routing rules. This reduces unnecessary processing, minimizes noise, and enforces logical separation in event-driven applications.

This section explores the different types of filters available in Azure Event Grid, how to combine them for powerful event routing, and how they contribute to the scalability, maintainability, and reliability of distributed event-based systems.

Why Filtering Matters

Without filtering, every subscription would receive all events published to the topic, leading to:

- **Increased load on event handlers**
- **Waste of compute resources**
- **Longer processing latency**
- **Security risks from irrelevant or sensitive data exposure**

With filtering, only events that match specific conditions are delivered to a subscription.

Types of Filters in Event Grid

Azure Event Grid supports three levels of filtering:

1. **Event Type Filtering**
2. **Subject Filtering**
3. **Advanced Filtering**

Filters are evaluated at the time of subscription. If an event does not meet the filter criteria, it is dropped before delivery—conserving bandwidth and compute.

Event Type Filtering

This is the simplest form of filtering. It matches events based on their eventType field.

Example

—included-event-types OrderPlaced OrderCancelled

Only events with eventType equal to OrderPlaced or OrderCancelled will be routed.

This is especially useful when a topic is publishing a wide variety of events and different consumers are interested in different event types.

Subject Filtering

Every Event Grid event has a subject field, which often represents the resource path or logical hierarchy of the event.

You can filter based on:

- subjectBeginsWith
- subjectEndsWith
- Both

Example

—subject-begins-with "/orders/"

—subject-ends-with "/created"

This would match events whose subjects start with /orders/ and end with /created, such as:

/orders/12345/created

/orders/uk/12345/created

Subject filters are string-based and do not support wildcards or regex.

Advanced Filtering

Advanced filtering allows you to build complex filter expressions on fields inside the data object or top-level event fields such as eventType, subject, or dataVersion.

Supported operators include:

- **Equals**
- **NumberGreaterThan**
- **NumberLessThan**
- **BoolEquals**
- **StringContains**
- **StringBeginsWith**
- **StringEndsWith**

JSON Example (CLI)

—advanced-filter data.total NumberGreaterThan 1000

—advanced-filter data.priority StringEquals High

This matches events where:

- data.total > 1000
- AND data.priority == "High"

JSON Example (ARM Template)

```
"advancedFilters": [
{
"key": "data.total",
"operatorType": "NumberGreaterThan",
"value": 1000
},
{
"key": "data.priority",
"operatorType": "StringIn",
"values": ["High", "Urgent"]
}
]
```

This ensures that only high-priority and large-value orders are delivered to the subscription.

Combining Filters

Filters can be combined in AND logic. If any filter fails, the event is discarded for that subscription.

To achieve OR behavior, use **multiple subscriptions** with different filters.

Example

1. Subscription A: data.priority = High
2. Subscription B: data.customerType = Enterprise

Each can deliver the event to different systems or the same endpoint with varied routing logic.

Using Filters with System Topics

Filters can also be applied to **system topics**. For example, when monitoring Blob Storage, you can filter by event type (Microsoft.Storage.BlobCreated) and subject (/containerA/).

az eventgrid event-subscription create \

—name blob-monitor \

—source-resource-id /subscriptions/.../storageAccounts/myStorage \

—subject-begins-with "/containerA/" \

—included-event-types Microsoft.Storage.BlobCreated

Best Practices for Filtering

1. **Use subject for hierarchical organization** (e.g., /orders/region/123).
2. **Use eventType to separate logical actions** (e.g., OrderCreated, OrderShipped).
3. **Use advanced filters for business logic** (e.g., order value, customer segment).
4. **Avoid over-filtering** that blocks critical events.
5. **Use multiple subscriptions** to implement OR-based logic

or broadcast patterns.

6. **Prefix subjects** consistently for predictable filtering (/app/service/action/id).

Example Scenario: Order Processing

Context

An e-commerce platform sends the following events:

{

"eventType": "OrderPlaced",

"subject": "/orders/uk/12345",

"data": {

"orderId": "12345",

"total": 1500,

"priority": "High",

"customerTier": "Gold"

}

}

Subscriptions

1. **Billing Service**

○ eventType = OrderPlaced

○ subjectBeginsWith = /orders/

○ data.total > 0

2. **Fraud Detection**

○ data.total > 1000

○ data.priority = High

3. **Marketing Analytics**

○ eventType in OrderPlaced, OrderCancelled

○ data.customerTier = Gold

Each subscription gets only the events it needs.

Implementing Filtering via Bicep

```
resource subscription 'Microsoft.EventGrid/eventSubscriptions@2022-06-15' = {

name: 'fraud-detector'

scope: topic

properties: {

destination: {

endpointType: 'WebHook',

properties: {

endpointUrl: 'https://fraud.myapi.com/handler'

}
```

```
}
filter: {
subjectBeginsWith: '/orders/',
includedEventTypes: ['OrderPlaced'],
advancedFilters: [
{
key: 'data.total',
operatorType: 'NumberGreaterThan',
value: 1000
},
{
key: 'data.priority',
operatorType: 'StringEquals',
value: 'High'
}
]
}
}
}
```

Diagnostic Monitoring of Filtered Events

Use **Azure Monitor** to track:

- Number of filtered events per subscription
- Delivery failures due to misconfigured filters
- Event drop rates from misapplied logic

Enable diagnostic settings on the topic or domain to log matched and unmatched events for further analysis.

Handling Schema Drift

Filtering assumes a consistent schema. If the schema changes:

- Filters may fail silently.
- No events will be delivered unless corrected.

Recommendation:

- Use **schema versioning** via the dataVersion field.
- Validate filters post-deployment.
- Implement a monitoring subscription to catch unmatched events.

Summary

Azure Event Grid's advanced routing and filtering features allow architects and developers to define precise, scalable, and secure event-driven systems. By thoughtfully applying event type, subject, and advanced filters, teams can reduce noise, enforce responsibility boundaries, and optimize downstream performance.

Filtering is not just a convenience—it's a core capability that enables real-time systems to scale safely and responsibly. In the next section, we will explore how to secure these event flows using encryption, private networking, authentication policies, and diagnostics, ensuring compliance and protection in mission-critical environments.

Event Grid Security and Monitoring

Security and monitoring are critical to building production-grade systems on Azure Event Grid. As a central component of event-driven architectures, Event Grid must be secured against unauthorized access, accidental data leaks, and abuse. It must also be observable at every level to ensure reliable operations, rapid troubleshooting, and continuous improvement. This section outlines how to secure Event Grid topics, domains, and subscriptions, how to enforce access controls and encryption, and how to monitor system health, diagnose issues, and ensure compliance with enterprise governance policies.

Securing Event Grid Infrastructure

Securing Event Grid starts with a **defense-in-depth approach**—combining authentication, network controls, encryption, and operational governance.

Authentication and Authorization

1. Azure Active Directory (Azure AD)

Azure Event Grid supports **role-based access control (RBAC)** via Azure AD, enabling fine-grained identity and access management.

Common Roles:

- EventGrid Data Sender – for publishing events
- EventGrid Event Subscription Contributor – for managing subscriptions
- Reader – for read-only access to configurations

Example: Granting sender access

```
az role assignment create \

—assignee <principal-id> \

—role "EventGrid Data Sender" \

—scope
/subscriptions/<sub-id>/resourceGroups/<rg>/providers/
Microsoft.EventGrid/topics/orders-topic
```

Always prefer **Managed Identities** for compute services (e.g., Azure Functions, App Services) over manual secrets.

2. Shared Access Signature (SAS) Keys

Custom topics and domain topics support **SAS authentication** via keys. These are useful for:

- Quick setup
- Integrating legacy systems

Best Practices:

- Use **short-lived tokens**
- Rotate keys regularly
- Store keys in **Azure Key Vault**

3. Webhook Validation

When using **custom webhooks** as event handlers, Event Grid sends a **validation handshake** request. Your endpoint must echo back the validationCode within a few seconds.

Example (C#):

```
public IActionResult Post([FromBody] JObject request)
{
if (request["validationCode"] != null)
{
return Ok(new { validationResponse = request["validationCode"].ToString() });
}
// Handle real event
}
```

Without proper validation, the subscription will not activate.

Network Security

1. Private Endpoints (Premium Tier)

For maximum security, Event Grid supports **Private Link**, allowing access to custom topics and domains from within a virtual network.

az network private-endpoint create \

—name eventgrid-private \

—resource-group myRG \

—vnet-name myVNet \

—subnet mySubnet \

—private-connection-resource-id /subscriptions/.../Microsoft.EventGrid/topics/orders-topic \

—group-id topic

This ensures events do not traverse the public internet.

2. IP Filtering and Firewalls

You can restrict which IP ranges can publish or subscribe to Event Grid endpoints.

Recommendation:

- Use IP filtering for webhook destinations

- Use firewall rules on storage accounts and function apps
- Combine with NSGs for layered control

3. VNet Integration for Subscribers

Make sure subscribers such as Azure Functions or App Services are integrated with VNets to receive events securely.

Encryption

Encryption in Transit

All Event Grid traffic is encrypted using **TLS 1.2+**. Clients should enforce this by disabling older protocols.

Encryption at Rest

Event Grid encrypts event data at rest using **Microsoft-managed keys** by default. Premium Event Grid allows **Customer-Managed Keys (CMKs)** using Azure Key Vault.

Bicep Example:

```
resource eventgridTopic 'Microsoft.EventGrid/topics@2022-06-15' = {
name: 'secure-topic'
location: 'eastus'
properties: {
inputSchema: 'EventGridSchema'
```

```
publicNetworkAccess: 'Disabled'
encryption: {
keySource: 'Microsoft.KeyVault'
keyVaultProperties: {
keyVaultUri: 'https://myvault.vault.azure.net/'
keyName: 'eventgrid-key'
keyVersion: 'latest'
}
}
}
}
```

CMKs are mandatory for organizations under strict compliance requirements (HIPAA, PCI-DSS, etc.).

Diagnostics and Monitoring

Visibility into event delivery, failures, and latency is essential to ensure system reliability and SLA compliance.

Diagnostic Settings

Enable **diagnostic logs** on topics, domains, and system topics.

```
az monitor diagnostic-settings create \
—name eventgrid-logs \
```

—resource
/subscriptions/<sub-id>/resourceGroups/<rg>/providers/
Microsoft.EventGrid/topics/orders-topic \

—workspace <log-analytics-id> \

—logs '[{"category": "DeliveryFailures", "enabled": true}, {"category": "AllMetrics", "enabled": true}]'

Categories include:

- DeliveryFailures
- PublishFailures
- SubscriptionValidation
- AllMetrics

Metrics to Monitor

- **PublishSuccessCount**: Successful event publishing operations
- **DeliveryAttemptCount**: Delivery retries
- **DeliveryFailureCount**: Failed deliveries
- **DeadLetteredEventCount**: Events moved to DLQ

Azure Monitor Alerts

Set up alerts to notify when delivery issues occur.

az monitor metrics alert create \

—name event-failures-alert \

—resource /subscriptions/.../Microsoft.EventGrid/topics/orders-topic \

—condition "total DeliveryFailureCount > 10" \

—description "High event delivery failure rate"

Dead Lettering

When events cannot be delivered (e.g., due to subscriber downtime), Event Grid retries delivery for 24 hours using exponential backoff. After that, undelivered events can be **dead-lettered** to a **storage blob container**.

az eventgrid event-subscription create \

—name orders-sub \

—source-resource-id /subscriptions/.../topics/orders-topic \

—endpoint https://myhandler.com \

—deadletter-destination blobstorage \

—storage-account myStorage \

—storage-container deadletters

Use **Lifecycle Management** on the blob container to auto-delete old dead-letter data.

Subscriber Reliability

To prevent Event Grid delivery failures:

- Ensure **high availability** of webhook endpoints

- Return **HTTP 2xx** status codes promptly
- Avoid long processing times—use asynchronous processing if needed
- Handle **validation events** gracefully
- Implement **health checks** and redundancy

Governance and Compliance

For enterprise environments, apply the following:

- Use **Azure Policy** to enforce encryption and public access settings.
- Integrate with **Azure Defender for Cloud** to get recommendations and threat alerts.
- Apply **Tagging** for resource tracking and cost management.

Example: Policy to Deny Public Access

```
{
"if": {
"allOf": [
{
"field": "type",
"equals": "Microsoft.EventGrid/topics"
```

```
},
{
"field": "Microsoft.EventGrid/topics/publicNetworkAccess",
"equals": "Enabled"
}
]
},
"then": {
"effect": "deny"
}
}
```

Log Correlation and Tracing

To track a single event through a distributed system:

- Use a **correlation ID** (e.g., data.correlationId)
- Log correlation ID in all handlers
- Pass correlation context downstream (e.g., into Service Bus, Functions, or storage logs)

This allows you to diagnose issues, measure latency, and trace end-to-end flow.

Summary

Azure Event Grid offers a secure and observable foundation for building robust event-driven applications. With support for RBAC, encryption, network isolation, dead-lettering, and deep diagnostics, it meets the needs of both agile development and enterprise governance.

Security and monitoring are not optional—they are integral to achieving system trustworthiness and operational excellence. Whether you're handling financial transactions, telemetry from IoT devices, or customer actions in real time, protecting and auditing your event pipeline is essential.

The next chapter will dive into Azure Event Hubs, focusing on large-scale telemetry ingestion, stream processing, and real-time analytics pipelines to complement your Event Grid-based architecture.

Chapter 7: Harnessing Azure Event Hubs

Event Ingestion at Scale

In today's hyper-connected digital world, applications generate an enormous volume of telemetry, logs, and event streams in real time. Capturing, processing, and analyzing these high-throughput streams efficiently is essential to gaining insights, enforcing automation, and ensuring operational awareness. Azure Event Hubs is a fully managed, real-time data ingestion service designed to handle millions of events per second with low latency and high availability.

This section explores how Azure Event Hubs can be used for massive-scale ingestion of event data from diverse sources, including applications, IoT devices, infrastructure components, and external systems. It provides architectural considerations, configuration practices, ingestion patterns, and performance tuning strategies.

Understanding Azure Event Hubs

Azure Event Hubs is an event streaming platform as a service (PaaS) that acts as a highly scalable data pipeline for real-time analytics, telemetry processing, and streaming ingestion. It serves as the front door for event data entering Azure for processing, storage, or visualization.

Key Capabilities:

- High throughput: Ingest millions of events per second

- Low latency: Millisecond latency for real-time applications
- Retention: Store event data for up to 90 days
- Partitioned consumers: Parallel processing support
- Native integration: With Azure Stream Analytics, Databricks, Kafka, Functions, and more

---

Core Components

- **Event Producers**: Devices or services that send event data into the hub
- **Event Hub**: The central ingestion point (stream buffer)
- **Partitions**: Parallel processing lanes within the hub
- **Consumer Groups**: Independent readers of event streams
- **Event Receivers**: Services that process or forward ingested data

---

Setting Up an Event Hub Namespace

Before you can ingest events, create an **Event Hubs namespace** and one or more **event hubs** within it.

az eventhubs namespace create \

—name telemetry-namespace \

—resource-group myResourceGroup \

—location eastus \

—sku Standard

Next, create an event hub:

az eventhubs eventhub create \

—name sensor-data-hub \

—resource-group myResourceGroup \

—namespace-name telemetry-namespace \

—message-retention 7 \

—partition-count 4

Choosing the Right SKU

Azure Event Hubs offers three SKUs:

SKU	Throughput	Features
Basic	Limited	No capture, no VNet, no Kafka endpoint
Standard	Moderate	Supports capture, up to 20 TU
Premium	High	Dedicated clusters, VNet, encryption, higher scale

For production-scale ingestion (100k+ events/sec), use **Standard or Premium** tiers.

Event Producers: Sending Data to Event Hubs

You can ingest events via SDKs, REST APIs, or integrations.

Example: Using .NET SDK

```
var producerClient = new EventHubProducerClient(connectionString, "sensor-data-hub");

using EventDataBatch eventBatch = await producerClient.CreateBatchAsync();

eventBatch.TryAdd(new
EventData(Encoding.UTF8.GetBytes("{\"temp\": 21.3}")));

eventBatch.TryAdd(new
EventData(Encoding.UTF8.GetBytes("{\"temp\": 22.7}")));

await producerClient.SendAsync(eventBatch);
```

Batching Tips:

- Use CreateBatchAsync to optimize payloads
- Batch sizes reduce network calls and improve throughput

Partitioning for Scale

Each event hub is divided into **partitions**. Producers can specify a **partition key** to ensure ordering for a stream (e.g., by device ID).

```
await producerClient.SendAsync(eventBatch, new SendEventOptions {

PartitionKey = "device-123"

});
```

Partitioning Guidelines:

- Use consistent hashable keys (e.g., user ID, device ID)
- Avoid sending all data to a single partition
- The number of partitions should match or exceed the expected number of concurrent consumers

---

Kafka-Compatible Ingestion

Azure Event Hubs supports the **Kafka protocol** out of the box—no code changes required for existing Kafka producers.

Configure Kafka clients with:

- Broker: <namespace>.servicebus.windows.net:9093
- SASL mechanism: PLAIN
- Security protocol: SASL_SSL

This allows you to reuse Kafka tooling while benefiting from Azure's PaaS reliability.

High-Throughput Configuration

For workloads exceeding 1 MB/s or 1,000 events/sec per partition:

- Use **Throughput Units (TU)** in Standard (up to 20 TUs per namespace)
- In Premium, use **Capacity Units (CU)** for higher guaranteed throughput

- Enable **Auto-Inflate** to scale up based on load

```
az eventhubs namespace update \
—name telemetry-namespace \
—resource-group myResourceGroup \
—enable-auto-inflate true \
—maximum-throughput-units 20
```

Capture for Long-Term Storage

Enable **Event Hubs Capture** to automatically store ingested data in Azure Storage or Azure Data Lake.

```
az eventhubs eventhub update \
—name sensor-data-hub \
—resource-group myResourceGroup \
—namespace-name telemetry-namespace \
—enable-capture true \
—capture-interval 300 \
—capture-size-limit 314572800 \
—destination-name EventHubArchive \
—storage-account <storage-id> \
—blob-container my-container
```

Use captured data for:

- Offline batch processing
- Forensics and auditing
- Replaying streams for testing or compliance

Receiving Events

Use the **EventProcessorClient** in Azure SDKs to read events from partitions with checkpointing.

```
var processor = new EventProcessorClient(
blobContainerClient, // for checkpointing
EventHubConsumerClient.DefaultConsumerGroupName,
eventHubConnectionString,
eventHubName
);
processor.ProcessEventAsync += async (args) =>
{
var data = Encoding.UTF8.GetString(args.Data.Body.ToArray());
Console.WriteLine($"Received: {data}");
await args.UpdateCheckpointAsync(args.CancellationToken);
};
await processor.StartProcessingAsync();
```

Checkpointing ensures you don't reprocess the same event on restart.

Integrating with Azure Services

- **Azure Functions**: Trigger-based processing of events
- **Stream Analytics**: Real-time analytics and transformation
- **Azure Data Explorer**: Time-series queries and dashboards
- **Synapse Pipelines**: Batch ingestion and machine learning

Example: Azure Function Binding

```
[FunctionName("TelemetryProcessor")]
public static void Run([EventHubTrigger("sensor-data-hub", Connection = "EventHubConnectionAppSetting")] string[] events, ILogger log)
{
foreach (string eventData in events)
{
log.LogInformation($"Event received: {eventData}");
}
}
```

Monitoring and Diagnostics

Enable diagnostic logs and metrics to monitor ingestion performance:

- IncomingBytes
- IncomingMessages
- ThrottledRequests
- CaptureBacklog

Use **Azure Monitor** for alerting and **Log Analytics** for queries.

Example alert:

```
az monitor metrics alert create \
—name high-throughput-alert \
—resource <eventhub-namespace-id> \
—condition "total IncomingBytes > 1073741824" \
—description "More than 1 GB ingested in last interval"
```

Best Practices

- **Use batching** and compression to reduce network overhead
- **Design partition keys** for scalability and ordering
- **Enable capture** for downstream analytics
- **Use retry policies** and backpressure mechanisms

- **Implement checkpointing** for at-least-once or exactly-once processing
- **Integrate with managed identity** for secure producer and consumer access
- **Segment workloads** using consumer groups

Summary

Azure Event Hubs provides a powerful, scalable, and flexible backbone for real-time event ingestion across distributed systems. With its support for high-throughput data streaming, native Kafka compatibility, automatic capture, and seamless integration with Azure analytics and serverless tools, Event Hubs is ideal for any application needing robust telemetry or event pipeline support.

The next section will dive into how to architect your Event Hub partitions and consumer groups using best practices for parallelism, ordering, and reliable stream processing.

Partitioning and Consumer Groups

Azure Event Hubs is engineered to support massive scale, but handling such scale effectively depends on how you architect the ingestion and processing of events. Partitioning and consumer groups are two fundamental design constructs in Event Hubs that enable high-throughput, parallel processing while preserving message ordering when required. This section covers the in-depth mechanics, design patterns, and best practices around partitioning and consumer groups, including how they influence performance, fault tolerance, and data flow in real-time systems.

Understanding Partitions

A **partition** in Azure Event Hubs is a data structure that acts as an independent stream within an event hub. When events are sent to an event hub, they are distributed across partitions either by a round-robin strategy or based on a provided partition key. This partitioning model is what allows Event Hubs to support concurrent producers and consumers while offering scalable throughput and ordered processing within each partition.

Characteristics of Partitions

- Immutable append-only log
- Events are added sequentially
- Each partition has its own **offsets** and **sequence numbers**
- Messages are retained based on configured retention (up to 90 days)
- Reading from a partition is stateful and requires **checkpointing**

Choosing the Number of Partitions

When you create an event hub, you specify the number of partitions. This number is immutable after creation.

Considerations:

- Each partition supports up to **1 MB/s or 1000 messages/sec** of ingress and egress
- Choose partition count based on:
  - Expected throughput
  - Number of concurrent consumers
  - Requirements for ordering

Minimum rule: Number of partitions ≥ number of concurrent consumers required

```
az eventhubs eventhub create \
—name telemetry-stream \
—namespace-name myNamespace \
—resource-group myRG \
—partition-count 8
```

Partition Planning Example:

If you anticipate:

- 2 million events/hour (~555 events/sec)
- 4 types of processing consumers (e.g., analytics, fraud detection, alerting, logging)

Then, 8 partitions is a safe baseline to support:

- Parallel processing
- Separation of workloads
- Scalability buffer

Sending with Partition Keys

If you want to ensure that related events (e.g., from the same user, device, or session) arrive in the same partition and maintain order, use a **partition key**.

```
var options = new SendEventOptions {

PartitionKey = "device-9823"

};

await producerClient.SendAsync(eventBatch, options);
```

Partition keys are hashed to assign events to partitions. The key itself is not stored—only used for deterministic routing.

Partition Key Use Cases:

- IoT devices
- User sessions
- Application regions or services

Avoid using:

- UUIDs or overly random keys

- Global partition keys (single partition hot-spotting)

Direct Partition Targeting

You can also explicitly target a partition, but this disables automatic load balancing and should only be used in advanced scenarios (e.g., testing, ordered stream replication).

```
var eventData = new EventData(Encoding.UTF8.GetBytes("..."));

await producerClient.SendAsync(new[] { eventData }, new SendEventOptions {

PartitionId = "0"

});
```

Understanding Consumer Groups

A **consumer group** is a view (state, offset, and processing) of the event hub's data stream. Each consumer group operates independently and maintains its own position (via offset or sequence number) in each partition.

Default Consumer Group

Every event hub has a default consumer group called $Default. However, creating **dedicated consumer groups** for each logical processing pipeline is recommended.

```
az eventhubs eventhub consumer-group create \

—eventhub-name telemetry-stream \

—name analytics \
```

—namespace-name myNamespace \

—resource-group myRG

Scaling with Consumer Groups

Each consumer group allows **a set of consumers to independently process** the event stream. This supports:

- **Parallel pipelines** (e.g., storage, alerting, analytics)
- **Multiple teams** reading the same event data
- **Isolation of workloads** to avoid coordination across teams

Use Case Example:

Consumer Group	Function
$Default	Archival to Blob
analytics	Real-time dashboards
fraudcheck	Alerting abnormal patterns
alerts	Notification delivery

Each group independently reads the same data from partitions and can checkpoint its progress.

Processing Events from Partitions

To process events in a scalable and fault-tolerant way, use the **EventProcessorClient** SDK. This allows automatic partition balancing and fault recovery.

var processor = new EventProcessorClient(

```
blobContainerClient,
"analytics", // consumer group
eventHubConnectionString,
eventHubName
);
processor.ProcessEventAsync += async (args) => {
var data = Encoding.UTF8.GetString(args.Data.Body.ToArray());
await args.UpdateCheckpointAsync(args.CancellationToken);
};
await processor.StartProcessingAsync();
```

This abstracts:

- Partition ownership
- Checkpoint management
- Load balancing across hosts

Checkpointing and Offset Management

To avoid reprocessing or skipping events, Event Hubs consumers must **checkpoint**—recording the last successfully processed offset.

Checkpointing is typically implemented using:

- **Azure Blob Storage**

- **Azure Table Storage (legacy)**
- **Custom database**

Key Benefits:

- Resume from last known state after a crash or restart
- Maintain exactly-once or at-least-once guarantees depending on configuration

Tip:

Checkpoint frequently enough to avoid long replay windows, but not so often that it overloads storage.

Event Hub Scaling with Partitions and Consumers

Event Hubs supports high concurrency via **partitioned parallelism.** Each partition can be consumed by a **single consumer instance per consumer group at a time.**

To process all partitions in a consumer group:

- Deploy as many instances as partitions
- Use **EventProcessorClient** to distribute partitions among instances

Partition Ownership Example:

Instance	Partition
A	0, 1
B	2, 3

If instance B crashes, A takes over B's partitions automatically.

Monitoring Partitions and Consumers

Track these metrics via Azure Monitor:

- IncomingMessages: Total messages received
- OutgoingMessages: Messages read by consumers
- PartitionIds: View partition distribution
- ThrottledRequests: Signal of under-provisioned consumers

Enable **diagnostic logging** to get events like:

- Partition ownership changes
- Checkpoint writes
- Event delivery errors

Best Practices

- **Define consistent partition keys** to preserve ordering
- **Avoid partition key collisions** that lead to hot partitions
- **Use separate consumer groups** per service or team
- **Use EventProcessorClient** for dynamic scaling and reliability

- **Checkpoint frequently** to enable fault recovery
- **Monitor partitions** for uneven load or processing delays
- **Plan partitions** based on peak throughput, not averages

Summary

Partitioning and consumer groups are the foundation of scalable and resilient Event Hubs architectures. With partitions, Event Hubs delivers high parallelism and throughput while preserving order within each key space. With consumer groups, you can fan out processing pipelines across teams, services, or use cases, enabling true decoupling.

Mastering these concepts ensures that your real-time systems built on Event Hubs are not only performant and efficient, but also maintainable, observable, and future-proof. The next section will explore real-time analytics and stream processing using Azure Event Hubs as the ingestion backbone.

Real-Time Analytics and Stream Processing

As data becomes a strategic asset, the ability to analyze and act on event streams in real time is a competitive differentiator. Azure Event Hubs serves as the primary ingestion point for high-throughput, low-latency data streams, making it a foundational component in real-time analytics pipelines. However, ingestion alone is not enough. Real value is realized when data is transformed, enriched, filtered, and acted upon within milliseconds or seconds of arrival.

This is where real-time analytics and stream processing enter the equation.

This section focuses on how to connect Azure Event Hubs to various Azure services and open-source tools to process, transform, and analyze event data in real time. It explores native integrations, architectural patterns, performance considerations, and the operational lifecycle of real-time streaming applications.

Core Concepts of Stream Processing

Stream processing is the continuous, real-time processing of data streams as they are received. Unlike batch processing, which works with static datasets, stream processing enables:

- **Low-latency insights**
- **Near-instant decision-making**
- **Continuous computation**

Key goals include:

- Event transformation and enrichment
- Anomaly detection
- Trend analysis
- Aggregations and windowing
- Alerting and actions

Architectural Flow

A typical Azure-based real-time analytics pipeline using Event Hubs includes:

1. **Event Producers** – Apps, devices, or services sending data
2. **Event Hubs** – Ingests and buffers streaming data
3. **Stream Processors** – Azure Stream Analytics, Azure Databricks, Apache Flink, etc.
4. **Data Stores** – Azure Data Lake, Synapse, Cosmos DB, etc.
5. **Dashboards and Actions** – Power BI, alerts, machine learning models

---

Using Azure Stream Analytics (ASA)

Azure Stream Analytics is a fully managed, serverless stream processing engine that integrates seamlessly with Event Hubs. It supports SQL-like syntax for real-time transformations.

Connecting ASA to Event Hubs

```
az stream-analytics input create \

—resource-group myRG \

—job-name process-orders \

—name input-orders \

—type Stream \

—datasource eventhub \

—eventhub-namespace telemetryns \
```

```
—eventhub-name orders-hub \

—consumer-group analytics \

—shared-access-policy-name RootManageSharedAccessKey \

—shared-access-policy-key <key>
```

Sample Query

```
SELECT

System.Timestamp AS WindowEnd,

userId,

COUNT(*) AS OrderCount,

SUM(totalAmount) AS TotalSpent

FROM input-orders TIMESTAMP BY eventTime

GROUP BY userId, TumblingWindow(minute, 5)
```

This calculates per-user metrics over a 5-minute window.

Output to Azure SQL

```
az stream-analytics output create \

—job-name process-orders \

—name output-sql \

—datasource sql \

—server mydbserver \
```

```
—database mydb \

—table order_summary \

—user myadmin \

—password <password>
```

Using Azure Databricks for Advanced Analytics

For ML-based or complex transformation scenarios, Azure Databricks offers a scalable Spark environment.

Connecting Databricks to Event Hubs

Use the Spark Event Hubs connector:

```
event_hub_config = {

'eventhubs.connectionString':
sc._jvm.org.apache.spark.eventhubs.EventHubsUtils.encrypt("<EventHubC

}

df = spark.readStream \

.format("eventhubs") \

.options(**event_hub_config) \

.load()

from pyspark.sql.functions import *

json_df = df.selectExpr("cast(body as string) as
json").select(from_json("json", schema).alias("data")).select("data.*")
```

You can now perform transformations, joins, aggregations, or ML inference.

Sample Use Cases:

- Predictive maintenance
- Fraud detection
- Real-time product recommendations

Integrating with Azure Synapse for Mixed Workloads

Azure Synapse supports **Synapse Link for Event Hubs**, enabling hybrid real-time + batch analytics.

Pattern:

1. Ingest real-time events into Event Hubs
2. Use Synapse pipelines or Spark to process events
3. Join with historical data
4. Visualize results in Synapse Studio or Power BI

This model bridges operational analytics (real-time) and BI workloads (batch).

Event Hubs + Apache Flink or Kafka Streams

For organizations using open-source tools:

- Apache Flink offers powerful windowing, event-time processing, and exactly-once semantics.

- Kafka Streams can consume from Event Hubs (via Kafka protocol) for local transformations.

Example: Kafka Streams + Event Hubs

```
StreamsBuilder builder = new StreamsBuilder();

KStream<String, String> stream = builder.stream("orders");

KStream<String, Long> total = stream

.groupByKey()

.count()

.toStream();
```

Configure Kafka properties to point to your Event Hubs Kafka endpoint.

Event Hubs and Real-Time Dashboards

Use **Power BI Streaming Datasets** or **Azure Data Explorer Dashboards** to visualize live data.

Power BI Flow:

1. ASA outputs data to Power BI workspace
2. Live dashboard reflects stream updates in <5 seconds
3. Users get insights without refreshing the page

Alerting and Real-Time Actions

Trigger actions from stream processors:

- **Azure Functions**: Call when pattern matches (e.g., temperature > 100°C)
- **Logic Apps**: Send SMS, email, or push notifications
- **Webhooks**: Integrate with third-party tools (PagerDuty, Slack)

Example ASA Query with Alerting Output:

```
SELECT
deviceId,
AVG(temp) AS avgTemp
INTO alert-stream
FROM input-stream
GROUP BY TumblingWindow(second, 30), deviceId
HAVING avgTemp > 100
```

Monitoring Stream Pipelines

Monitor with:

- Azure Monitor
- ASA job metrics (e.g., InputEvents, LateEvents, WatermarkDelay)
- Databricks job dashboards
- Synapse Spark job history

Configure alerts for:

- Query failures
- Throttled Event Hub reads
- High watermark delays

Performance Tips

- Prefer **tumbling and hopping windows** over sliding when possible
- Use **late arrival tolerance** to handle network lag
- Scale ASA with **Streaming Units (SU)**
- Partition data smartly to prevent hot partitions
- Use checkpointing in Databricks/Flink for fault tolerance

Summary

Azure Event Hubs, when combined with real-time stream processing tools like Azure Stream Analytics, Databricks, and Apache Flink, becomes a powerful platform for ingesting, transforming, and analyzing event data at scale. Whether you are building fraud detection systems, customer analytics dashboards, or IoT telemetry pipelines, the flexibility and scalability of Event Hubs ensure that insights arrive in time to make a difference.

In the next section, we'll explore how to integrate Event Hubs with Azure Stream Analytics and Apache Kafka ecosystems, creating robust, scalable pipelines that power both real-time and long-term analytical workloads.

Integration with Azure Stream Analytics and Apache Kafka

To truly harness the value of Azure Event Hubs, you need to integrate it with processing engines that can ingest, analyze, and act on streaming data in near real time. Two of the most powerful tools in this domain are **Azure Stream Analytics (ASA)** and **Apache Kafka**. Azure Stream Analytics offers a fully managed solution for complex stream processing using a SQL-like language, while Apache Kafka and its ecosystem provide a robust open-source foundation for high-throughput event streaming, stream transformations, and distributed processing.

This section details the integration patterns, configuration approaches, best practices, and advanced use cases when combining Azure Event Hubs with ASA and Kafka—enabling enterprise-grade real-time data pipelines.

Why Integrate Event Hubs with ASA and Kafka?

Azure Event Hubs acts as a unified ingestion layer for telemetry, logs, metrics, transactions, IoT data, and more. However, the raw events need to be processed, filtered, aggregated, and routed. That's where Stream Analytics and Kafka-based tools step in.

Key Benefits of Integration:

- Real-time dashboards and anomaly detection

- Event transformation and enrichment
- Low-latency alerting and automation
- Stream data warehousing and long-term analytics
- Language flexibility: SQL (ASA), Java/Scala (Kafka Streams), Python (Flink)

Azure Stream Analytics Integration

Connecting ASA to Event Hubs

You can connect ASA to Event Hubs via input configuration either in the Azure Portal, CLI, ARM, or Bicep.

```
az stream-analytics input create \
—resource-group analyticsRG \
—job-name trafficAnalysis \
-name eventhub-input \
—type Stream \
—datasource eventhub \
—eventhub-namespace telemetry-hub-ns \
—eventhub-name traffic-events \
—consumer-group analytics \
—shared-access-policy-name RootManageSharedAccessKey \
```

```
—shared-access-policy-key <key>
```

Real-Time SQL Query Example

```
SELECT
deviceId,
AVG(speed) AS averageSpeed,
System.Timestamp AS windowEnd
INTO output-database
FROM eventhub-input
TIMESTAMP BY eventTime
GROUP BY deviceId, TumblingWindow(minute, 1)
HAVING averageSpeed > 120
```

This query calculates the average speed of vehicles and sends alert data when speeds exceed a threshold.

Common Outputs

- Azure SQL Database
- Blob Storage
- Power BI
- Azure Cosmos DB
- Azure Data Lake

- Event Hubs (for routing to downstream processors)

```
az stream-analytics output create \
—job-name trafficAnalysis \
—name alert-output \
—datasource sql \
—server sql-server.database.windows.net \
—database telematics \
—table alerts \
—user adminuser \
—password <password>
```

Advanced ASA Features

- **Temporal windowing** (tumbling, hopping, sliding)
- **Out-of-order tolerance** with LateArrival policy
- **Stream joins** across multiple inputs
- **User-defined functions** (C#/JavaScript)
- **Machine learning model integration** (ONNX)

Example: ML Scoring in Stream Analytics

```
SELECT
eventTime,
```

sensorId,

ML.Predict(scoreModel, temperature, pressure, vibration) AS anomalyScore

INTO anomalyOutput

FROM telemetryInput

Apache Kafka Integration via Event Hubs

Azure Event Hubs supports **Kafka protocol head**. This allows Kafka producers and consumers to work with Event Hubs **without any code changes**.

Kafka Client Configuration

```
bootstrap.servers=yourNamespace.servicebus.windows.net:9093

security.protocol=SASL_SSL

sasl.mechanism=PLAIN

sasl.jaas.config=org.apache.kafka.common.security.plain.PlainLoginModu
required \

username="$ConnectionString" \

password="Endpoint=sb://yourNamespace.servicebus.windows.net/;Sha
```

Using Kafka Producer

```
Properties props = new Properties();

props.put("bootstrap.servers",
"yourNamespace.servicebus.windows.net:9093");
```

```
props.put("key.serializer",
"org.apache.kafka.common.serialization.StringSerializer");

props.put("value.serializer",
"org.apache.kafka.common.serialization.StringSerializer");

Producer<String, String> producer = new
KafkaProducer<>(props);

producer.send(new ProducerRecord<>("orders", "orderId123",
"{\"orderTotal\": 299.99}"));
```

Kafka Streams and KSQL Use Cases

Kafka Streams and ksqlDB can be layered on top of Event Hubs for:

- Stateful aggregations
- Real-time joins and enrichments
- Filtering and anomaly detection

Kafka Streams Example

```
KStream<String, Order> orders = builder.stream("orders");

KStream<String, Double> highValueOrders = orders

.filter((key, order) -> order.getTotal() > 1000)

.mapValues(order -> order.getTotal());

highValueOrders.to("high-value-orders");
```

This will read from orders in Event Hubs and produce to high-value-orders, also hosted in Event Hubs.

Real-Time Lambda Architecture

Azure Event Hubs with ASA or Kafka supports a **Lambda Architecture** pattern:

- **Speed Layer**: Real-time insights via ASA or Kafka Streams
- **Batch Layer**: Raw event capture to Data Lake or Storage
- **Serving Layer**: Power BI, dashboards, alerting systems

This design ensures high accuracy, reprocessability, and resilience.

Performance Considerations

- Use **partition keys** in Kafka or Event Hubs to ensure ordered processing
- Tune **window sizes** and **latency tolerances** in ASA to balance timeliness vs. data completeness
- Enable **checkpointing** in both ASA and Kafka Streams to avoid reprocessing
- For high volume, use **Azure Managed Kafka (Confluent)** or **Premium Event Hubs**
- Use **parallel ASA streaming units (SU)** or **Kafka workers** to horizontally scale

---

Monitoring and Diagnostics

Monitor integration pipelines using:

- **ASA job metrics**: InputEvents, OutputEvents, LateEvents
- **Event Hub metrics**: IncomingBytes, ThrottledRequests
- **Kafka metrics** (via JMX exporters): Consumer lag, broker throughput
- **Azure Monitor logs**: Subscription delivery failures, job errors

Set up **alerts** for:

- ASA query runtime errors
- Kafka consumer lag spikes
- Event Hub throttling or backlog

Use Cases

1. **Fraud Detection**

   - Ingest card transactions via Event Hubs
   - Stream to ASA for pattern matching
   - Route flagged events to notification service

2. **IoT Sensor Monitoring**

◦ Ingest data via Kafka to Event Hubs

◦ Stream processing via ksqlDB

◦ Store results in Azure Data Explorer

3. **Clickstream Analysis**

◦ Real-time ingestion of website activity

◦ Process with Databricks or ASA

◦ Power dashboards and personalize UX

4. **Log Ingestion and Alerting**

◦ Syslogs via Kafka to Event Hubs

◦ ASA detects anomalies

◦ Output to SIEM and incident tools

Best Practices

- Use **Event Hubs with capture enabled** for replay capability

- Use **multiple consumer groups** for separation of concerns (analytics vs. monitoring)

- Prefer **Azure Stream Analytics** for rapid deployment and SLA-backed processing

- Use **Kafka integration** for open-source flexibility and complex topologies

- Always **checkpoint consumer offsets** to avoid duplicates and ensure idempotency

---

Summary

Integrating Azure Event Hubs with Azure Stream Analytics and Apache Kafka unlocks a world of real-time intelligence, from streaming dashboards and automated alerting to machine learning and business insights. ASA offers a fast path to productive stream analytics using a familiar SQL interface, while Kafka brings extensibility, advanced stream transformations, and integration with a rich ecosystem of distributed tools.

By combining these technologies, organizations can build modern data platforms that respond instantly to change, scale to handle massive input volumes, and deliver actionable insights in milliseconds. The next chapter will move from architecture to application, exploring real-world use cases across industries and how Event Hubs plays a pivotal role in operationalizing event-driven solutions.

Chapter 8: Real-World Use Cases and Case Studies

IoT Data Collection and Processing

The Internet of Things (IoT) has transformed industries by enabling billions of devices to generate real-time data that can be used for monitoring, automation, analytics, and intelligent decision-making. From manufacturing and logistics to smart agriculture and healthcare, IoT devices emit telemetry that needs to be collected, ingested, processed, and stored at scale. Azure provides a comprehensive platform for IoT data collection and processing, and Azure Event Hubs plays a central role in the architecture by acting as the ingestion backbone.

This section explores a full-scale real-world use case of building an IoT telemetry pipeline using Azure Event Hubs, including design decisions, integration patterns, processing strategies, scalability practices, and examples from actual implementations.

Use Case Overview

Scenario: A smart agriculture company has deployed thousands of environmental sensors across multiple farms. These sensors capture temperature, humidity, soil moisture, and light levels every 5 seconds. The objective is to ingest this data, process it in real time for anomaly detection, and store it for later analytics and compliance reporting.

Requirements:

- Handle over 10 million events/day

- Ensure sub-second ingestion latency
- Process data for alerting and control actions
- Store raw and aggregated data
- Visualize metrics and trends in real time
- Ensure security, scalability, and reliability

Architecture Overview

1. **Sensor Devices** – Publish telemetry data via MQTT or HTTPS
2. **IoT Hub** – Manages device connectivity and security
3. **Event Hubs** – Acts as a high-throughput telemetry ingestion buffer
4. **Stream Processing** – Azure Stream Analytics filters and aggregates data
5. **Data Storage** – Raw data is stored in Data Lake; aggregates in SQL
6. **Visualization** – Dashboards in Power BI, Grafana, or Azure Data Explorer
7. **Alerts** – Triggered via Logic Apps or Functions on anomalies

---

Ingestion with IoT Hub and Event Hubs

Azure IoT Hub integrates directly with Event Hubs-compatible endpoints. Internally, IoT Hub routes telemetry into a built-in Event Hub-compatible stream.

Configuration

az iot hub create \

—name smart-agriculture-hub \

—resource-group agriRG \

—sku S1 \

—partition-count 4

The built-in endpoint is accessed like an Event Hub:

"Endpoint=sb://iothub-ns-smart-agriculture-xxx.servicebus.windows.net/;SharedAccessKeyName=iothubowner;Shar ehub-smart-xxxx"

Devices publish telemetry to IoT Hub, which then forwards messages to the Event Hubs-compatible endpoint for downstream consumption.

Real-Time Processing with Azure Stream Analytics

ASA processes messages in near real time, performing transformations, filters, and windowed aggregations.

Example Query

SELECT

deviceId,

System.Timestamp AS WindowEnd,

AVG(temperature) AS AvgTemp,

```
AVG(soilMoisture) AS AvgMoisture

INTO aggregates-output

FROM telemetry-input TIMESTAMP BY eventTime

GROUP BY deviceId, TumblingWindow(minute, 1)
```

This aggregates telemetry every minute per device and stores the result in SQL for dashboarding.

Anomaly Detection Query

```
SELECT

deviceId,

temperature,

soilMoisture,

eventTime

INTO alert-output

FROM telemetry-input

WHERE temperature > 45 OR soilMoisture < 15
```

Anomalous readings are routed to Logic Apps to notify farm managers or trigger irrigation.

Storing Raw and Aggregated Data

To support both real-time and historical analysis:

- **Raw telemetry** is captured using Event Hubs Capture into **Azure Data Lake.**
- **Aggregates** are stored in **Azure SQL Database** or **Cosmos DB**.

Enabling Capture

```
az eventhubs eventhub update \
—resource-group agriRG \
—namespace-name agriNamespace \
—name telemetry-hub \
—enable-capture true \
—storage-account mylakeaccount \
—blob-container telemetry \
—capture-interval 300 \
—capture-size-limit 104857600
```

Captured data can be used by Synapse for batch processing or machine learning model training.

Real-Time Dashboards

Farm managers use **Power BI** or **Azure Data Explorer dashboards** to visualize trends.

Power BI Steps:

1. ASA outputs aggregates to SQL

2. Power BI refreshes dashboard every minute
3. Heatmaps display environmental metrics by region

For more scalable, live dashboards, **Azure Data Explorer (ADX)** can ingest events from Event Hubs and visualize them using Kusto queries.

Alerts and Actions

When conditions exceed thresholds, immediate actions are triggered.

Integration Options:

- **Azure Functions**: To trigger irrigation, ventilation, or lighting
- **Logic Apps**: To send emails, SMS, Teams alerts
- **Webhook Services**: To connect with external field control systems

Sample Logic App Trigger

1. ASA outputs anomaly to Event Hub
2. Event Grid routes event to Logic App
3. Logic App sends SMS using Twilio or Email using Office365

Scaling and Performance Optimization

Partition Planning

With 10,000+ devices, ensure at least 8-16 partitions to support parallel reads and writes. Use deviceId as the **partition key** for ordered ingestion and even load distribution.

Stream Analytics Scaling

Use **streaming units (SUs)** to scale ASA jobs.

```
az stream-analytics job update \
—job-name telemetryProcessing \
—resource-group agriRG \
—output-error-policy Drop \
—streaming-units 6
```

Monitor job health: input backlog, watermark delay, and output throttling.

Consumer Group Isolation

Use dedicated consumer groups for:

- ASA
- Capture/Storage
- Custom Analytics

- Alert Systems

This isolates workloads and allows independent scaling.

Security and Compliance

- Use **per-device identity** in IoT Hub with SAS keys or certificates
- Secure Event Hubs with **RBAC or Managed Identity**
- Enable **private endpoints** for IoT Hub and Event Hubs
- Encrypt data at rest with **CMK integration**
- Implement **data retention** and **access policies** for compliance (e.g., ISO, GDPR)

Operational Considerations

- Set up **Azure Monitor alerts** for failed ASA jobs or Event Hub throttling
- Enable **diagnostic logs** for Event Hubs, IoT Hub, and ASA
- Use **Log Analytics** to trace data flow and detect failures
- Schedule **data retention policies** on storage containers

Real-World Outcome

Customer: AgriSense Technologies

Impact:

- Reduced water usage by 35% through automated irrigation
- Prevented crop loss through early frost and heat detection
- Gained real-time visibility across 20+ farms
- Improved compliance reporting with secure, auditable data storage

---

Summary

This IoT use case illustrates how Azure Event Hubs, in conjunction with IoT Hub, ASA, and storage services, enables robust and scalable telemetry pipelines. From ingestion to visualization, this architecture supports real-time action and long-term insights, providing clear business value in operational efficiency, sustainability, and responsiveness.

The next section will explore financial systems and how Event Hubs supports secure, auditable, and real-time transaction processing in banking and fintech environments.

Financial Systems and Transaction Alerts

Modern financial systems demand unparalleled reliability, scalability, and security. From high-frequency trading to fraud detection and customer notifications, financial institutions rely heavily on real-time data processing to ensure business continuity, meet regulatory compliance, and deliver superior customer experiences. Azure Event Hubs is ideally positioned to serve as a foundational component in this space, enabling the ingestion and routing of millions of events per second from disparate sources into a unified stream processing pipeline.

This section details a comprehensive use case of using Azure Event Hubs to build a transaction alerting system within a financial institution. It covers ingestion architecture, security enforcement, event routing, real-time alerting, regulatory compliance, and integration with fraud analytics systems.

Use Case Overview

Scenario: A retail banking institution wants to implement a system that ingests and analyzes customer transactions across all channels—ATMs, online banking, point-of-sale terminals, and mobile apps. The system must generate real-time alerts for suspicious activity, send customer notifications for critical transactions, and archive transaction data for compliance and audits.

Key Requirements:

- Process over 50 million transactions daily
- Detect anomalies in sub-second latency
- Route events to multiple systems (fraud engine, CRM, storage)
- Maintain end-to-end encryption and access control
- Integrate with real-time dashboards and historical analytics
- Ensure full observability and failure recovery

Architecture Components

1. **Transaction Producers** – Core banking systems, ATM software, mobile apps, etc.
2. **Event Hubs Namespace** – Ingests transactions via a single, centralized hub
3. **Consumer Groups** – Separate processing streams for fraud analysis, alerts, storage
4. **Azure Stream Analytics / Apache Kafka Streams** – Detects anomalies
5. **Azure Functions** – Sends SMS/email notifications
6. **Azure Data Lake + Synapse Analytics** – For storage, compliance, and BI
7. **SIEM and Monitoring Systems** – Ensure visibility and audit readiness

---

Event Hubs Setup

Namespace and Event Hub Creation

az eventhubs namespace create \

—name banking-namespace \

—resource-group finRG \

—location eastus \

—sku Standard

az eventhubs eventhub create \

—name transactions-hub \

```
—namespace-name banking-namespace \
—resource-group finRG \
—message-retention 7 \
—partition-count 16 \
—enable-capture true \
—capture-interval 300 \
—capture-size-limit 524288000 \
—destination-name compliance-storage \
—storage-account bankingarchive \
—blob-container transactions
```

This configuration supports high-throughput ingestion and compliance-grade event retention.

Transaction Format

Each transaction message is standardized as a JSON object:

{
"transactionId": "tx-908afc0",
"customerId": "cust-10892",
"amount": 450.75,
"currency": "USD",
"timestamp": "2025-05-09T16:45:12Z",

```
"channel": "POS",
"location": "NYC",
"merchant": "XYZ Retail",
"type": "purchase",
"deviceId": "term-583"
}
```

Producers are configured to send events in this format using Azure SDKs, Kafka connectors, or REST APIs.

Fraud Detection via Stream Analytics

Azure Stream Analytics jobs continuously process events to identify fraud signals:

Sample ASA Query

```
SELECT
customerId,
COUNT(*) AS txCount,
SUM(amount) AS totalSpent,
System.Timestamp AS windowEnd
INTO potentialFraudStream
FROM transactionsInput TIMESTAMP BY timestamp
GROUP BY customerId, TumblingWindow(minute, 2)
```

HAVING txCount > 5 AND totalSpent > 3000

This detects when a customer performs >5 high-value transactions within 2 minutes—potentially fraudulent behavior.

Alerting and Notification System

Detected anomalies are routed to an **Event Hub consumer group** for Azure Functions to handle.

Azure Function Binding Example

```
[FunctionName("SendTransactionAlert")]

public static void Run(

[EventHubTrigger("transactions-hub", ConsumerGroup = "alerts")] string[] events,

ILogger log)

{

foreach (var evt in events)

{

var transaction = JsonConvert.DeserializeObject<Transaction>(evt);

if (transaction.Amount > 1000)

{

SendSmsAlert(transaction.CustomerId, transaction.Amount);

}
```

```
}

}
```

The function calls Twilio, SendGrid, or Logic Apps to notify customers of suspicious or high-value activity.

Storing Data for Compliance

Financial regulations (e.g., SOX, PCI-DSS, PSD2) require full transaction traceability. Event Hubs Capture stores all transactions in **Azure Data Lake**.

Benefits:

- Immutable, time-stamped storage
- Partitioned by date/customer/location
- Integrated with **Azure Synapse** for queries and reporting
- Long-term archival with **storage lifecycle rules**

Integration with SIEM Tools

Security teams require visibility into transaction anomalies and processing errors. Event Hubs and ASA diagnostics are forwarded to:

- **Microsoft Sentinel**
- **Splunk**

- **QRadar**
- **Elastic Stack**

az monitor diagnostic-settings create \

—name eventhub-logs \

—resource "/subscriptions/xxx/resourceGroups/finRG/providers/Microsoft.EventHub/namespaces/banking-namespace" \

—workspace <logAnalyticsId> \

—logs '[{"category": "AllMetrics", "enabled": true}]'

Kafka Integration for Internal Teams

Internal systems already using Apache Kafka can send/receive events via **Kafka-compatible Event Hubs**.

Producer Properties:

bootstrap.servers=banking-namespace.servicebus.windows.net:9093

security.protocol=SASL_SSL

sasl.mechanism=PLAIN

sasl.jaas.config=org.apache.kafka.common.security.plain.PlainLoginModule required \

username="$ConnectionString" \

password="Endpoint=sb://banking-namespace.servicebus.windows.net/;Sh

This allows seamless ingestion from Java-based fraud engines, rule processors, or CRM systems.

Dashboards and Visualization

- ASA aggregates are stored in SQL or Cosmos DB
- Dashboards built in **Power BI** or **Grafana**
- Metrics include:
  - Volume by channel
  - High-risk merchant patterns
  - Location-based anomalies
  - Hourly activity spikes

Real-time Power BI streaming datasets provide up-to-the-minute visibility to risk managers and branch operators.

Resilience and Failover

- **Auto-inflate** enables scaling Event Hubs dynamically under peak load
- ASA supports **streaming unit scaling**
- **EventProcessorClient** handles **partition failover** in consumers
- Use **dead-letter queues** to route unprocessable messages
- Re-ingestion workflows ensure no data is lost even during outages

---

Security Practices

- All events encrypted **in transit (TLS)** and **at rest (Azure-managed or customer-managed keys)**
- Managed Identity used for secure access between Event Hubs, ASA, and Functions
- Network access restricted via **Private Link**
- Role-based access control (RBAC) assigned per processing role

---

Real-World Example

Client: FinNow Digital Bank

Impact:

- Reduced fraud losses by 63% in Q1 using stream-based anomaly detection
- Reduced SMS latency from 30s (batch model) to <3s with Event Hubs and Functions
- Enabled full PSD2 audit logging with Event Hubs Capture
- Cut infrastructure costs by migrating from self-managed Kafka to Azure Event Hubs

---

Summary

Event Hubs provides a scalable, secure, and efficient backbone for ingesting and routing financial transaction data. When combined with Azure Stream Analytics and Functions, it enables powerful real-time monitoring, fraud detection, and alerting pipelines. Financial institutions can meet strict compliance requirements while simultaneously delivering better customer protection and operational agility.

In the next section, we'll explore how these same messaging capabilities empower media and gaming platforms to manage high-velocity events, synchronize gameplay, and enhance real-time interactivity at global scale.

Media and Gaming: Handling High-Velocity Events

The media and gaming industries are among the most demanding in terms of real-time data processing. Online multiplayer games, live sports streaming, video analytics, real-time chat, telemetry collection, and content personalization all require the handling of massive volumes of events with extremely low latency. Azure Event Hubs is well-suited for such workloads, offering the ability to ingest millions of events per second, integrate with stream processing engines, and deliver scalable fan-out to a wide range of consumers.

This section explores how media and gaming platforms use Azure Event Hubs to power interactive experiences, measure performance, moderate content, deliver live updates, and perform real-time analytics.

Use Case Overview

Scenario: A game development company operates a large-scale multiplayer online game with millions of concurrent users. Players interact in real time across different geographic regions, and the system must:

- Collect player telemetry (movement, actions, device stats)
- Detect cheating behavior
- Match players based on skill and behavior
- Provide real-time leaderboards
- Analyze game server health and player drop-offs
- Monitor content for moderation in real-time voice and chat channels

Simultaneously, the company operates a video streaming platform with real-time viewer metrics, adaptive bitrate decisions, and content recommendations.

Ingestion Strategy with Event Hubs

Given the high-velocity nature of player events and streaming data, the architecture must scale elastically and ensure low-latency delivery.

Event Producers:

- Game clients (PC, console, mobile)

- Game servers and session controllers
- CDN edge nodes
- Chat and voice engines
- Video player SDKs
- Backend services for payments, achievements, and matchmaking

Key Event Types:

{
"eventType": "PlayerMovement",
"playerId": "user-72836",
"sessionId": "sess-a7f2c9",
"timestamp": "2025-05-09T21:00:00Z",
"coordinates": { "x": 304, "y": 190 },
"zone": "arena-east",
"latency": 42,
"device": "xbox-series-x"
}

Each event is sent to an **Event Hub namespace** with partitioning based on sessionId or zone.

Architecture Overview

1. **Azure Event Hubs** – Central ingestion layer with high throughput and partitioned streams
2. **Azure Functions** – Lightweight processing for player session updates and metrics routing
3. **Azure Stream Analytics** – Processes real-time game telemetry and viewer data
4. **Cosmos DB / Redis** – For fast session state storage
5. **Azure Data Explorer / Synapse** – For real-time dashboards and aggregate queries
6. **Event Grid** – Triggers moderation workflows and streaming alerts
7. **Azure DevOps / GitHub Actions** – Push live events to deployed servers during patch cycles

---

Real-Time Telemetry Collection

Each game client sends telemetry at a regular interval (e.g., 10 events per second). Event Hubs ingests:

- Player movement and actions
- Performance metrics (FPS, ping, CPU usage)
- Input telemetry (controller latency, button combinations)

This data enables developers to optimize gameplay, detect abnormal performance, and study engagement.

Processing with Stream Analytics

```
SELECT

playerId,

MAX(latency) AS MaxLatency,

AVG(latency) AS AvgLatency,

COUNT(*) AS EventCount

INTO player-metrics

FROM game-telemetry

TIMESTAMP BY timestamp

GROUP BY playerId, TumblingWindow(second, 10)
```

This provides near-real-time latency statistics for each player.

Cheat Detection and Behavior Analysis

Combining input timing, impossible movement patterns, or abnormal scores allows ASA or Apache Flink to detect potential cheating.

Example: Detecting Impossible Movement

```
SELECT

playerId,

MIN(coordinates.x) AS StartX,

MAX(coordinates.x) AS EndX,
```

DATEDIFF(second, MIN(timestamp), MAX(timestamp)) AS Duration

INTO suspicious-movement

FROM player-movements

GROUP BY playerId, TumblingWindow(second, 5)

HAVING ABS(EndX - StartX) > 500 AND Duration < 1

If a player teleports across the map too quickly, the event is flagged and forwarded to moderators.

Real-Time Leaderboards and Matchmaking

Event Hubs feeds a leaderboard service that aggregates game scores and achievements.

- Stream updates via ASA into **Cosmos DB**
- Use change feed to update **SignalR live dashboards**
- Push leaderboard updates to players every 1-3 seconds

Matchmaking services consume events to dynamically rank players and create fair matches based on:

- Skill score
- Latency profile
- Behavioral risk score

Content Moderation in Chat and Voice

Using real-time transcription and profanity filters, Event Hubs routes flagged audio and chat messages to moderation systems.

- Azure Cognitive Services performs speech-to-text
- Azure Functions evaluates text for flagged content
- Event Grid triggers moderation workflows
- Messages violating policies are blocked or reported

This ensures compliance with online safety regulations and enhances community experience.

Video Streaming Analytics

For the media platform, Event Hubs collects:

- Playback starts and stops
- Bitrate change events
- Buffering durations
- Viewer location and CDN edge info
- Ad impressions and skips

ASA Query for Buffering Analysis

SELECT

location,

```
COUNT(*) AS BufferingEvents,

AVG(bufferDuration) AS AvgBufferTime

INTO playback-insights

FROM video-metrics

WHERE eventType = 'Buffering'

GROUP BY location, TumblingWindow(minute, 5)
```

This drives real-time operational dashboards for network engineering teams.

Game Patch Coordination and LiveOps

During live events or content updates:

- Event Hubs captures install events and patch download progress
- Event Grid notifies servers of version compliance issues
- A deployment system (Azure DevOps, GitHub Actions) uses this telemetry to phase rollouts
- Azure Functions triggers on low adoption or update errors

This enables safe and reactive patch cycles, reducing downtime and user frustration.

Scaling and Resilience

- Use **partition keys** for sessions or zones to maintain order
- Scale Event Hubs with **Auto-Inflate** and monitor IncomingMessages
- Deploy multiple consumer groups: analytics, alerts, moderation, ops
- Enable **Event Hubs Capture** to preserve telemetry for replays and training ML models
- Store long-term data in **Data Lake** for historical analysis and player behavior modeling

---

Monitoring and Observability

- **Azure Monitor**: Tracks Event Hub metrics (IncomingBytes, ThrottledRequests)
- **Application Insights**: Logs latency from event publishing to processing
- **Log Analytics**: Correlates game events with server logs
- **Dashboards**: Real-time dashboards show:

○ Active sessions

○ Region-based latency

○ Viewer counts and buffering spikes

◦ Leaderboard top movers

Real-World Outcome

Customer: StellarPlay Games

Impact:

- Increased player retention by 24% using personalized leaderboard updates
- Reduced cheating reports by 81% via real-time pattern recognition
- Enabled live event moderation for millions of concurrent players
- Improved viewer experience by dynamically adjusting bitrate based on telemetry
- Delivered interactive experiences (e.g., live trivia during streams) with <1s latency

---

Summary

For media and gaming companies, delivering real-time interactive experiences at global scale demands robust data streaming infrastructure. Azure Event Hubs serves as a critical foundation, enabling low-latency telemetry ingestion, distributed processing, and intelligent routing. Integrated with Azure Stream Analytics, Functions, and monitoring tools, Event Hubs empowers developers to build resilient, reactive, and engaging digital experiences.

The next section explores how these technologies are applied in the healthcare sector to enable secure, compliant, and real-time communication in patient care and hospital operations.

Healthcare: Secure Real-Time Notifications

In the healthcare sector, timely, reliable, and secure communication is paramount. From notifying physicians of critical lab results to synchronizing telemetry from patient monitoring devices, real-time messaging has the potential to save lives, streamline workflows, and improve patient outcomes. However, healthcare systems must also navigate strict regulatory frameworks such as HIPAA, GDPR, and ISO 27001, which demand the highest standards of data security and auditability.

Azure Event Hubs provides a scalable and secure foundation for real-time healthcare event ingestion and distribution. Paired with services such as Azure Functions, Event Grid, and Azure Monitor, Event Hubs enables robust notification workflows, telemetry analysis, and medical alerting systems—all while enforcing enterprise-grade compliance and governance.

Use Case Overview

Scenario: A national healthcare provider operates a network of hospitals, clinics, and mobile health units. Each facility generates real-time events such as:

- Patient admission, discharge, and transfer (ADT)
- Critical lab and imaging results
- Alerts from bedside monitors and wearable IoT devices

- Staff requests and workflow triggers
- Appointment and medication reminders

The objective is to build a secure, scalable real-time notification system that delivers the right data to the right clinician, at the right time, on the right device—while ensuring compliance with privacy regulations and maintaining full traceability.

Architecture Components

1. **Event Producers** – EHR systems, lab devices, bedside monitors, mobile apps
2. **Azure Event Hubs** – Central stream ingestion layer
3. **Azure Stream Analytics / Azure Functions** – Real-time filtering, transformation, and enrichment
4. **Azure Logic Apps / SignalR** – Delivery of messages to staff dashboards and mobile devices
5. **Azure Monitor and Sentinel** – Observability and security intelligence
6. **Azure Data Lake / SQL / Cosmos DB** – Long-term storage, audit logging, and data exploration

---

Event Ingestion Design

Each department (radiology, labs, ICU, pharmacy) emits domain-specific events, standardized in HL7 FHIR or custom JSON schemas.

Sample Event Payload

```
{
```

```
"eventType": "LabResultCritical",
"patientId": "pt-20498",
"timestamp": "2025-05-09T11:42:00Z",
"testType": "Troponin I",
"value": 7.6,
"unit": "ng/mL",
"referenceRange": "0.00 - 0.04",
"location": "ER Room 3",
"clinicianId": "dr-1092"
}
```

Events are routed to Event Hubs with a partitionKey such as patientId or facilityId to maintain ordering and scalability.

```
az eventhubs eventhub create \
—name clinical-events \
—namespace-name healthcare-ns \
—resource-group healthcareRG \
—partition-count 8 \
—message-retention 3
```

Real-Time Notification Flow

Critical Result Alerting with Azure Functions

1. Event is published to Event Hubs
2. Azure Function triggers on critical-results consumer group
3. The function validates payload, enriches with patient data, and routes to notification service

```
[FunctionName("CriticalResultHandler")]

public static void Run(

[EventHubTrigger("clinical-events", ConsumerGroup = "critical-results")] string[] events,

ILogger log)

{

foreach (var e in events)

{

var result = JsonConvert.DeserializeObject<LabResult>(e);

if (result.Value > 5.0) {

SendSecureNotification(result.ClinicianId, $"CRITICAL: {result.TestType} = {result.Value} ng/mL");

}

}

}
```

Delivery methods may include:

- Secure mobile push (via Azure Notification Hubs)
- SMS with PHI redacted
- In-app dashboards via SignalR
- Email to organizational inbox (if approved)

Patient Monitoring and IoT Telemetry

Wearables and bedside monitors stream telemetry every few seconds (e.g., heart rate, blood pressure, oxygen saturation).

Ingestion and Processing

- Devices send data to IoT Hub → forwards to Event Hubs
- Stream Analytics aggregates over short windows
- Azure Functions fire alerts when thresholds are breached

```
SELECT
patientId,
AVG(heartRate) AS avgHR,
MAX(heartRate) AS maxHR,
System.Timestamp AS timestamp
```

INTO alertStream

FROM telemetryInput TIMESTAMP BY timestamp

GROUP BY patientId, TumblingWindow(second, 10)

HAVING maxHR > 130 OR avgHR > 110

Alerts are routed to nursing stations and care teams.

Appointment Reminders and Workflow Triggers

Event Hubs receives patient appointment events from the EHR system:

{

"eventType": "AppointmentScheduled",

"patientId": "pt-9038",

"timestamp": "2025-05-10T15:00:00Z",

"location": "Outpatient West Wing",

"department": "Cardiology"

}

Logic Apps listens to these events to:

- Send SMS/email reminders
- Trigger preparation workflows (e.g., room assignment)
- Update patient portals

This reduces no-shows and improves patient satisfaction.

Compliance and Security

Healthcare data handling demands strict controls:

Encryption

- TLS 1.2+ for all in-transit data
- At-rest encryption using Microsoft- or customer-managed keys
- CMK support for Event Hubs (via Key Vault integration)

Authentication

- All services use **Managed Identities**
- Event Hubs protected by **RBAC**, not shared access keys
- Custom APIs require **OAuth2 with AAD**

Network Isolation

- Event Hubs and all processors operate with **Private Endpoints**
- VNet integration prevents public exposure
- Azure Firewall and NSGs enforce access policies

Auditing and Logging

- Diagnostic settings send Event Hub logs to **Azure Monitor**
- **Log Analytics** tracks dropped messages, failed function executions
- Alerts notify on unusual throughput patterns or throttling

High Availability and Disaster Recovery

- Event Hubs configured with **Geo-disaster recovery namespaces**
- ASA jobs run in **availability zones** to tolerate regional faults
- Critical events are **dually published** to a secondary Event Hub in another region
- Functions and Logic Apps are deployed in **active-active mode**

Analytics and Reporting

- ASA aggregates are written to **Azure SQL** for hospital dashboards
- Raw telemetry is stored in **Data Lake** for clinical studies

• Cosmos DB used for operational lookup and real-time queries

• Synapse Analytics provides long-term trend insights (e.g., ER response times, lab turnaround)

Example: Emergency Response Notification

1. Ambulance telemetry indicates a cardiac event in transit
2. Event sent via IoT Hub → Event Hubs → ASA
3. ASA routes event to Event Grid, triggers alert to cardiologist
4. Cardiologist views ECG preview via secure app before patient arrives
5. Emergency room is prepped in real-time

This workflow shortens response times and improves outcomes.

Real-World Impact

Healthcare System: UnityHealth National Services

Results:

• Reduced critical lab result notification time from 12 minutes to under 2 minutes

• Increased clinician response rates by 57% through mobile alerts

• Improved compliance with internal SLA benchmarks for emergency communications

- Enabled real-time telemetry visibility across over 30 facilities

---

Summary

Healthcare organizations face unique challenges in building real-time systems—balancing speed with compliance, and flexibility with security. Azure Event Hubs, when implemented with best practices in identity, encryption, and network controls, provides a HIPAA-aligned platform for secure, real-time event handling. Whether for patient monitoring, staff alerts, or system coordination, it empowers healthcare providers to act with precision, speed, and confidence—ultimately saving lives.

The next chapter will focus on operationalizing your Azure messaging systems: how to monitor, troubleshoot, and maintain event-driven applications at scale.

Chapter 9: Monitoring, Troubleshooting, and Maintaining Azure Messaging Systems

Setting Up Alerts and Metrics

Effective monitoring is a foundational element of any resilient messaging system. In Azure, where messaging services such as Event Hubs, Event Grid, and Service Bus operate at massive scale and often underpin critical workflows, the ability to detect anomalies, track performance, and proactively resolve issues is essential. This section explores how to set up metrics, logs, and alerts for Azure messaging services using tools such as Azure Monitor, Log Analytics, Application Insights, and custom telemetry.

We will detail key metrics to track, strategies for setting up alerts, integration patterns with incident management systems, and the best practices for observability in a production-grade event-driven architecture.

Why Monitoring Matters

Without effective monitoring and alerting, even small disruptions in a messaging system can lead to:

- Data loss or duplication
- Service degradation
- Broken workflows
- Delayed decision-making

- Compliance risks

Monitoring ensures that operations teams and developers have visibility into both system health and message flow characteristics.

Core Azure Monitoring Components

Azure offers a robust observability stack, including:

- **Azure Monitor**: Unified platform for metrics, logs, and alerts
- **Log Analytics**: Query engine and data workspace for telemetry
- **Application Insights**: Performance and telemetry tracking for apps
- **Azure Diagnostics**: Resource-specific event streams
- **Azure Alerts**: Rules to notify and trigger automation

Metrics to Monitor in Messaging Systems

Azure Event Hubs

Metric	Description
IncomingMessages	Number of events received per interval
IncomingBytes	Total volume of data ingested
OutgoingMessages	Events delivered to consumers
ThrottledRequests	Requests blocked due to quota limits
CapturedBytes	Data captured to storage (if enabled)
DeadLetteredMessages	Messages moved to the dead-letter queue

Azure Service Bus

Metric	Description
ActiveMessages	Messages in active state in a queue/topic
DeadLetterMessages	Messages moved to DLQ due to delivery failures
IncomingRequests	Total number of send/receive requests
ThrottledRequests	Requests throttled due to limits
Size	Total size of the queue or topic in bytes

Azure Event Grid

Metric	Description
DeliveredEvents	Successfully delivered events
FailedDeliveries	Events that failed all delivery attempts
MatchedEvents	Events that matched subscription filters
PublishSuccessCount	Events successfully published
DeliveryLatency	Time from publication to delivery

Enabling Diagnostic Settings

To access metrics and logs, diagnostic settings must be configured on each messaging resource.

```
az monitor diagnostic-settings create \

—name messaging-logs \

—resource
/subscriptions/<sub-id>/resourceGroups/<rg>/providers/
Microsoft.EventGrid/topics/my-topic \

—workspace <logAnalyticsId> \

—logs '[{"category": "AllMetrics", "enabled": true}, {"category":
"DeliveryFailures", "enabled": true}]'
```

Set retention policies and categories based on business requirements. Categories typically include:

- AllMetrics
- OperationalLogs
- DeliveryFailures
- DeadLetterEvents

Creating Alerts

Alerts allow you to respond to anomalies and issues before they impact users.

Example: Alert for High Dead Letter Count

```
az monitor metrics alert create \

—name high-dlq-alert \

—resource
/subscriptions/<sub-id>/resourceGroups/<rg>/providers/
Microsoft.ServiceBus/namespaces/my-ns/queues/orders \

—condition "total DeadLetterMessages > 100" \

—description "More than 100 messages in DLQ" \

—action-group ops-alert-group
```

Example: Alert for Event Hub Throttling

```
az monitor metrics alert create \

—name eh-throttle-alert \

—resource
/subscriptions/<sub-id>/resourceGroups/<rg>/providers/
Microsoft.EventHub/namespaces/telemetry-ns \

—condition "total ThrottledRequests > 10" \

—description "Throttling detected on Event Hub" \

—action-group ops-alert-group
```

Integrating with Incident Management Tools

Use Azure Action Groups to forward alerts to:

- **Email/SMS**

- **Webhook endpoints**
- **ITSM connectors (e.g., ServiceNow, PagerDuty)**
- **Logic Apps or Azure Functions**

az monitor action-group create \

—name ops-alert-group \

—resource-group alerts-rg \

—short-name ops \

—action email ops-team ops@example.com \

—action webhook incident-handler https://webhook.service/notify

This ensures that alerts integrate into existing incident workflows and escalation chains.

Building Dashboards

Azure Monitor Workbooks and Grafana (Azure Managed Grafana) provide real-time dashboards to visualize metrics.

Example Panels:

- **Event Hubs Throughput**: Line chart of IncomingMessages by partition
- **Service Bus Health**: Gauge of active vs. DLQ messages
- **Event Grid Success Rate**: Pie chart of delivered vs. failed

- **Latency Breakdown**: Box plot of Event Grid DeliveryLatency per subscription

These dashboards should be shared across ops, engineering, and product teams.

Log Queries with Kusto (KQL)

Use Log Analytics with KQL to explore operational data.

Example: Failed Deliveries in Event Grid

```
AzureDiagnostics

| where ResourceType == "EVENTGRIDTOPICS"

| where Category == "DeliveryFailures"

| summarize count() by bin(TimeGenerated, 5m), EventSubscriptionId
```

Example: DLQ Growth in Service Bus

```
AzureDiagnostics

| where EntityName_s == "payments"

| where Category == "ServiceBusDeadletterMessages"

| summarize max(TotalMessages) by bin(TimeGenerated, 10m)
```

Queries can be saved and scheduled for automated reports or anomaly detection.

Best Practices

- **Tag resources** for filtering in alerts and reports (env:prod, service:orders)
- **Set up alerts for both thresholds and absence of expected data**
- **Implement synthetic monitoring** to validate message delivery end-to-end
- **Use CorrelationId** to trace message flow through services
- **Monitor cold starts or high function latency** in consumer functions
- **Continuously test alerting configuration** to avoid silent failures

---

Cost Management Considerations

- Logs and metrics incur costs—tune retention and granularity
- Use **log sampling** and **filters** to exclude noise
- Group alerts using **dynamic thresholds** to reduce alert fatigue

---

Summary

Robust monitoring and alerting are non-negotiable in production-grade messaging systems. Azure provides all the building blocks necessary to achieve deep observability into message throughput, failures, and system health. By proactively tracking key metrics, setting up alerts, and leveraging log analytics, teams can ensure the reliability, performance, and security of their event-driven architectures.

The next section will guide you through diagnosing specific system failures and bottlenecks in Azure messaging solutions and show you how to systematically troubleshoot problems when they occur.

Diagnosing Failures and Bottlenecks

No system is immune to failures, and in event-driven architectures where components are loosely coupled and asynchronous by design, identifying the root cause of issues can be particularly challenging. Failures can occur at any stage in the message lifecycle—from the producer to the messaging service to the consumer—and manifest as dropped messages, unexpected latency, processing delays, or undelivered events. Diagnosing these issues effectively requires a structured approach that leverages telemetry, logging, and systemic patterns of behavior.

This section provides a comprehensive guide to diagnosing failures and bottlenecks in Azure messaging systems, including Azure Service Bus, Event Hubs, and Event Grid. We will explore how to interpret metrics, analyze logs, correlate event traces, and apply best practices for root cause analysis.

Categories of Failures and Bottlenecks

1. **Producer-side issues**

○ Throttled or rejected sends

○ Serialization errors

○ Network timeouts

2. **Messaging platform failures**

○ Internal throttling

○ Dead-lettering

○ Partition overload

3. **Consumer-side problems**

○ Message lock expiration

○ Function timeouts or cold starts

○ Incomplete processing

4. **Downstream system failures**

○ Storage unavailability

○ External API delays

○ Message replay loops

Diagnosing Event Hubs Issues

Symptoms

- Event ingestion drops intermittently
- High ThrottledRequests metric
- Event latency increases beyond SLA

Step-by-step Diagnostic Approach

1. **Check Namespace Metrics**

az monitor metrics list \

—resource /subscriptions/xxx/resourceGroups/rg/providers/Microsoft.EventHub/namespaces/telemetry-ns \

—metric ThrottledRequests IncomingMessages IncomingBytes

If ThrottledRequests > 0, increase throughput units or investigate producer misbehavior.

1. **Examine Partition Utilization**

Use Azure Monitor or Workbooks to visualize per-partition metrics.

High concentration of events in a single partition indicates poor partition key strategy.

1. **Verify Auto-Inflate Settings**

Ensure auto-inflate is enabled:

```
az eventhubs namespace update \
—name telemetry-ns \
—resource-group rg \
—enable-auto-inflate true \
—maximum-throughput-units 20
```

1. **Check Capture Pipeline**

Look for capture errors:

```
AzureDiagnostics
| where Category == "CaptureErrors"
| summarize count() by bin(TimeGenerated, 5m), ActivityId
```

Diagnosing Service Bus Failures

Common Symptoms

- Messages remain unprocessed
- Dead-letter queue fills rapidly
- Function triggers fail intermittently

Checklist

1. **Dead-letter Queue (DLQ) Inspection**

```
az servicebus queue show \
```

—name orders \

—namespace-name bus-namespace \

—resource-group rg

Check deadLetterMessageCount.

Use Service Bus Explorer or custom receivers to view DLQ contents and properties.

1. **Review Lock Duration and Message Handling**

If consumers fail to complete processing before lock expiry, messages may reappear.

```
{
"LockDuration": "00:01:00",
"MaxDeliveryCount": 10
}
```

Review logs for exceptions like MessageLockLostException.

1. **Analyze Application Insights for Consumers**

Look for function cold starts, timeout exceptions, and handler errors.

```
requests
| where name contains "ServiceBusTrigger"
| summarize avg(duration), count() by cloud_RoleName, resultCode
```

1. **Enable Auto-Scaling or Prefetch**

Use prefetchCount in SDK to reduce message retrieval overhead.

Diagnosing Event Grid Delivery Failures

Symptoms

- Events not reaching subscribers
- Subscriptions move to "dead-letter" state
- Delivery retries exceed maximum

Actions

1. **Check Delivery Logs**

AzureDiagnostics

| where Category == "DeliveryFailures"

| project TimeGenerated, EventSubscriptionId, ErrorMessage

Common issues:

- Subscriber endpoint timeout (HTTP 408)
- Authentication failures (HTTP 401/403)
- Invalid endpoint (HTTP 404)

1. **Validate Subscriber Availability**

Use curl, Application Insights, or availability tests to ensure the destination is reachable.

curl -i https://api.myendpoint.com/webhook

1. **Check Subscription Filters**

Events may not be delivered if they do not match the subject or event type filters.

Use:

az eventgrid event-subscription show \

—name my-subscription \

—source-resource-id /subscriptions/.../topics/my-topic

1. **Inspect Dead-Letter Storage**

Events failing delivery permanently can be found in the configured dead-letter blob container.

Correlating Events End-to-End

Use a correlationId in message headers or body to track event flow:

- Add to ApplicationProperties in Service Bus or Event Hub
- Use EventGridEvent.correlationId or define a custom field
- Pass through consumer logic and log in every handler

Query example:

traces

| where customDimensions.correlationId == "abc-123-def"

| project timestamp, message, operation_Name

This enables full flow analysis across producers, messaging fabric, and consumers.

Network and Authentication Troubleshooting

TLS/Connection Errors

- Ensure firewall rules allow port 5671 (AMQP) or 443 (HTTPS)
- Check VNet integration and NSGs for connectivity issues

Token Expiry or Misconfigured Credentials

- Use Managed Identity to avoid secret rotation errors
- Log authentication failures via SDK telemetry

Application Code Debugging

Use Azure Application Insights or OpenTelemetry SDKs:

- Record Request, Dependency, and Exception telemetry
- Instrument message lifecycle: send → enqueue → dequeue → process

Function App Example:

```
var telemetry = new DependencyTelemetry("ServiceBus", "orders", "process");

telemetry.Timestamp = DateTime.UtcNow;

telemetry.Duration = stopwatch.Elapsed;

telemetry.Success = success;

telemetry.Context.Operation.Id = correlationId;

telemetryClient.TrackDependency(telemetry);
```

Best Practices for Troubleshooting

- **Use structured logging**: Include message metadata (correlation ID, timestamps, event type)
- **Enable verbose SDK logging**: For example, ServiceBusClientOptions.Diagnostics
- **Isolate retry logic**: Use retry policies separate from core logic
- **Replay messages** from DLQ or capture for regression testing
- **Document thresholds and alerts**: Make expected behavior observable

---

Summary

Diagnosing failures in Azure messaging systems requires layered visibility, from infrastructure metrics to application telemetry. By systematically analyzing metrics, logs, and event flows—and correlating them across producers, messaging services, and consumers—you can efficiently detect root causes and mitigate operational disruptions. This diagnostic capability is essential for maintaining trust in real-time systems, especially in mission-critical domains.

The next section will focus on applying continuous improvement strategies to refine performance, increase fault tolerance, and evolve messaging architectures proactively.

Continuous Improvement Strategies

In the dynamic landscape of distributed systems, especially those built around messaging and event-driven architecture, maintaining operational excellence is not a one-time task. It is a continuous journey of measurement, refinement, and evolution. To ensure that Azure-based messaging infrastructures remain resilient, performant, and aligned with business needs, organizations must adopt a culture of continuous improvement. This involves iterating on processes, tuning system behavior, adapting architecture patterns, and implementing feedback mechanisms that close the loop between operations, development, and users.

This section presents a structured approach to continuous improvement for Azure messaging systems such as Event Hubs, Service Bus, and Event Grid. It outlines methodologies, automation practices, feedback loops, and organizational processes that support ongoing enhancement in reliability, scalability, observability, and cost-efficiency.

Measurement-Driven Iteration

At the heart of continuous improvement is measurement. Without quantifiable indicators of performance, it's impossible to know what to optimize or whether a change had a positive impact.

Key Performance Indicators (KPIs):

- **End-to-end latency** (event published → consumed)
- **Message processing success rate**
- **Dead-letter message trends**
- **Function or consumer error rates**
- **Partition and consumer group utilization**
- **Cost per message/event processed**
- **Availability/downtime incidents**

These KPIs should be tracked and reviewed periodically via dashboards and reports. Establish baseline values for comparison and flag anomalies through alerting systems.

Implementing Feedback Loops

Feedback loops allow teams to respond to operational data in near real-time or through retrospectives.

Operational Feedback

- Event Grid DeliveryFailed logs can trigger auto-suppression of faulty subscribers.

- Service Bus DeadLetterMessages count can launch automated DLQ inspection tools.

- Event Hub ThrottledRequests can trigger auto-scaling or throughput unit escalation.

Development Feedback

- Include logs from downstream consumers in performance dashboards.

- Use Application Insights or OpenTelemetry to measure processing durations by version or deployment.

- Correlate incidents with recent deployments via deployment annotations.

```
az monitor metrics alert create \
—name "HighProcessingLatency" \
—resource <function-app-id> \
—condition "avg Duration > 2000" \
—description "Function processing time exceeds 2s average"
```

Architecture Refactoring

Over time, systems must evolve to handle changing traffic patterns, new features, or infrastructure limits. Refactoring helps:

- Reduce coupling

- Improve scalability

- Increase developer velocity
- Enhance resilience

Common Refactoring Triggers:

- DLQs growing consistently → consider dead-letter analysis automation
- Consumer group contention → redesign consumer-to-partition mapping
- High failure rate in Event Grid → add queue-based buffer before subscribers
- Complex function code → split logic into micro-consumers or durable orchestrators

Techniques:

- Introduce **fan-in** or **fan-out** via Azure Functions or Logic Apps
- Migrate heavy consumers to **Durable Functions** or **Azure Container Apps**
- Replace brittle endpoints with **queue-backed retries**
- Convert static routes to **Event Grid advanced filters**

Scaling Tuning

Scaling should be dynamic and based on consumption metrics, not static assumptions.

Service Bus Example:

- Monitor ActiveMessages count and auto-scale consumer pods accordingly.
- Use prefetchCount tuning to reduce latency.

```
var processor = new ServiceBusProcessorOptions
{
MaxConcurrentCalls = 16,
PrefetchCount = 32,
AutoCompleteMessages = false
};
```

Event Hubs Example:

- Enable auto-inflate
- Balance partitions with appropriate partitionKey
- Deploy consumers in proportion to partition count

Stream Analytics:

- Adjust Streaming Units (SUs) based on lag and throughput
- Monitor WatermarkDelay and LateInputEvents

az stream-analytics job update \

—job-name process-stream \

—resource-group streamRG \

—streaming-units 6

Operational Playbooks and Automation

When an issue occurs, time spent diagnosing and recovering manually can cost the business. Playbooks codify resolution steps and prepare teams for rapid response.

Example Playbooks:

- **Event Hub Partition Hotspot**:

1. Analyze IncomingMessages per partition

2. Validate partitionKey logic in producer

3. Redistribute or hash by new key

- **DLQ Growth**:

1. Inspect DLQ messages

2. Route to staging environment

3. Replay with enhanced validation

- **Event Grid Latency Spike**:

1. Check endpoint responsiveness
2. Trigger fallback to alternate subscriber
3. Log failure context and incident ticket

Automate playbook execution via Azure Automation, Logic Apps, or custom Functions triggered on diagnostics.

Developer Enablement and Observability

Engineers need access to the right data at the right time to troubleshoot and improve the system.

Strategies:

- Create self-service dashboards with App Insights, Log Analytics, and Azure Workbooks
- Use **distributed tracing** with correlation IDs from producer to consumer
- Automate error classification: transient vs. permanent vs. code logic
- Provide simulators to replay event flows in dev/test environments

```
traces
| where customDimensions.eventType == "OrderCreated"
```

```
| summarize avg(duration), max(duration) by cloud_RoleName
```

Cost Optimization

Messaging systems at scale can accrue significant costs. Ongoing cost review ensures efficiency.

Optimization Methods:

- Reduce retention time for short-lived events
- Disable capture where archival is unnecessary
- Consolidate Event Hub namespaces where appropriate
- Scale down Function App plans during low-usage periods
- Evaluate use of **Basic vs. Standard vs. Premium SKUs**

Use Azure Cost Analysis to generate usage reports segmented by:

- Messaging service
- Environment
- SKU or feature usage
- Region

Governance and Compliance Reviews

Include messaging systems in regular compliance reviews. Validate:

- Diagnostic logs and alerts are properly retained

- Encryption keys (CMKs) are rotated
- RBAC roles follow least privilege principles
- Audit trails exist for all DLQ purges or message replays

Regular Postmortems and RCA

After any incident, conduct a blameless postmortem that includes:

- Timeline of events
- Contributing factors
- Gaps in observability
- Preventative and detective controls
- Remediation and long-term actions

Publish findings internally to support shared learning and prevention.

Summary

Continuous improvement in Azure messaging systems requires more than just monitoring and reaction—it demands an organizational mindset that embraces iteration, automation, and feedback. By combining real-time observability with strategic tuning and operational discipline, teams can ensure their messaging architectures evolve to meet tomorrow's demands while delivering reliability, performance, and efficiency today.

The next chapter explores how emerging technologies, including AI and evolving messaging standards, are shaping the future of real-time cloud messaging.

Chapter 10: Future Trends in Cloud Messaging and Events

Emerging Technologies and Standards

The landscape of cloud messaging and event-driven architecture continues to evolve rapidly, driven by demands for higher performance, greater reliability, increased interoperability, and tighter integration with data analytics and AI. As cloud-native platforms become the default foundation for building modern distributed systems, new technologies and standards are emerging that reshape how developers architect and scale messaging systems.

This section examines the most significant trends and innovations poised to impact the future of Azure messaging ecosystems and the broader cloud messaging landscape. These include protocol standardization, the rise of event mesh architectures, the convergence of messaging and streaming paradigms, and advances in event modeling and schema management.

The Rise of Open Standards and Interoperability

Historically, messaging systems have been fragmented by proprietary protocols and vendor-specific semantics. This has made integration complex and vendor lock-in a persistent challenge. However, there's a clear industry trend toward **open standards** that enable interoperability across platforms and ecosystems.

CloudEvents

CloudEvents is a CNCF-backed specification that standardizes the format of event metadata to ensure consistent routing, parsing, and handling of events across services.

Example CloudEvent JSON:

```
{
"specversion": "1.0",
"type": "com.example.object.deleted",
"source": "/storage/containers/images",
"id": "C234-1234-1234",
"time": "2025-05-09T15:00:00Z",
"datacontenttype": "application/json",
"data": {
"filename": "sample.jpg"
}
}
```

Azure Event Grid supports CloudEvents natively, and Event Hubs and Service Bus can interoperate with CloudEvents through transformation layers or API gateways.

AMQP 1.0

Azure Service Bus and Event Hubs both support **AMQP 1.0**, a standardized binary protocol that ensures efficient transport and supports advanced messaging patterns such as transactions, sessions, and message replay.

AMQP is increasingly becoming a baseline for secure, high-performance messaging across vendors and cloud platforms.

Event Mesh and Decentralized Eventing

As organizations adopt microservices, Kubernetes, and hybrid cloud architectures, the limitations of centralized event brokers are becoming apparent. This is driving the emergence of **event mesh** architectures—distributed systems of interconnected brokers that can publish and subscribe to events across boundaries.

Key characteristics:

- **Global routing** based on topic or content filters
- **Service discovery** for event producers and consumers
- **Built-in transformation and mediation**
- **Location-aware delivery** (e.g., send to nearest regional cluster)

Azure Implementation Strategies:

- Use **Event Grid Domains** and **Topics** to manage publisher-specific routing

- Implement cross-region **Event Hub replication** with custom routing
- Adopt **Service Bus Geo-disaster recovery** to support failover in mesh topologies
- Connect on-premises brokers (e.g., RabbitMQ, IBM MQ) to Azure via **Hybrid Connections** or **Azure Relay**

The adoption of event mesh allows for more scalable, resilient, and flexible architectures where producers and consumers evolve independently.

Convergence of Messaging and Streaming

Traditional messaging systems like Service Bus have historically emphasized durability, ordering, and delivery guarantees, while streaming platforms like Event Hubs have prioritized high-throughput and temporal event analysis.

There is a growing trend to **unify these paradigms**:

- **Streaming with guarantees**: Event Hubs supports exactly-once processing through checkpointing and Kafka semantics
- **Message queues with observability**: Service Bus metrics and logging now provide near-real-time insights into flow and performance
- **Stream-native microservices**: Azure Container Apps with Dapr bindings for Event Hubs and Service Bus allow services to natively react to events

This convergence enables developers to focus on business logic without needing to make hard trade-offs between throughput and reliability.

Schema Registries and Event Contract Governance

As event-driven systems scale, managing schema evolution becomes a critical challenge. Inconsistent payloads, undocumented formats, and incompatible consumers are major sources of failure.

Emerging practices include:

- **Schema-first design** using OpenAPI or JSON Schema
- **Azure Schema Registry** integration with Event Hubs and Kafka
- **Backward and forward compatibility checks** as part of CI/CD
- **Versioned contracts** with semantic versioning

Azure's Schema Registry, a feature of **Azure Event Hubs**, allows producers to register payload schemas and consumers to validate against them, enabling safer deployments and decoupled development.

```
az schemaregistry schema register \
—name userEvent \
—schema-group customerEvents \
—definition @userEvent.avsc \
—format Avro
```

This reduces incidents related to bad payloads and accelerates integration.

Serverless and Reactive Event Processing

Event-driven applications are increasingly built using **serverless** technologies for their auto-scaling, pay-per-use pricing, and low operational overhead.

Trends:

- **Function chaining** via Durable Functions or Azure Logic Apps
- **Reactive programming models** using Observables and RxJS
- **Stateful workflows** with Event Grid triggers and Logic Apps
- **Low-latency streaming analytics** using Azure Stream Analytics or Azure Data Explorer

This paradigm enables use cases like:

- Real-time fraud detection
- Personalized push notifications
- Adaptive content delivery
- Self-healing infrastructure via telemetry feedback loops

Edge Event Processing and 5G Integration

With the expansion of 5G networks and IoT proliferation, there's a shift toward **processing events at the edge**, reducing round-trip latency and offloading central systems.

Edge processing characteristics:

- Low-latency detection and decision-making (e.g., in factory automation)
- Preprocessing at the gateway level using Azure IoT Edge
- Local routing and buffering of telemetry
- Integration with Event Hubs for downstream streaming

Azure Percept and Azure Stack Edge allow event producers and filters to operate on-premises or at edge locations, forwarding only essential data to the cloud.

AI-Augmented Event Systems

The integration of AI and ML models into messaging workflows is becoming mainstream. These models assist in:

- **Predictive routing** (e.g., prioritizing alerts by risk score)
- **Anomaly detection** in telemetry
- **Natural language event classification** (e.g., from support tickets or chatbots)
- **Automated incident response**

Integration points:

- Azure ML models called from Azure Functions
- Event Hub streams feeding into Synapse ML pipelines
- Classification of events in real time via Azure Cognitive Services

This allows systems to become more intelligent and adaptive, responding not just to events, but to inferred patterns and predicted outcomes.

Sustainability and Energy Efficiency

Environmental impact is becoming a key metric for system design. Messaging systems contribute to energy usage through:

- Always-on consumers
- Over-retention of messages
- Redundant message replays

Strategies for improvement:

- Use **Auto Scaling** and **Consumption Plans** in Functions
- Implement **TTL policies** for messages and data retention
- Analyze system idle patterns and turn off nonessential resources

- Streamline processing with **content-based filtering** at the ingress point

By aligning with sustainability goals, cloud messaging systems can reduce costs and contribute to environmental responsibility.

Summary

The future of cloud messaging is shaped by interoperability, intelligent automation, decentralized topologies, and developer-centric experiences. Azure is evolving to support these trends through enhanced support for open standards like CloudEvents and AMQP, advanced features like schema governance and edge processing, and seamless integration with AI and analytics platforms.

These innovations will enable architects to build responsive, resilient, and cost-effective event-driven systems that not only meet today's requirements but are prepared for tomorrow's challenges. The next section will explore how artificial intelligence is further enhancing messaging systems through predictive processing and real-time adaptive behavior.

Role of AI and Machine Learning in Real-Time Systems

Artificial Intelligence (AI) and Machine Learning (ML) are increasingly shaping how real-time systems operate, especially in cloud-native environments. Messaging systems—once focused solely on reliable delivery—are now evolving to become intelligent event-processing platforms capable of responding not only to current events but also to patterns, predictions, and inferred outcomes. In Azure, the convergence of messaging services like Event Hubs, Event

Grid, and Service Bus with AI tools such as Azure Machine Learning, Cognitive Services, and Synapse ML is enabling a new generation of smart, adaptive, and proactive applications.

This section explores how AI/ML can be integrated with Azure messaging services to unlock new capabilities in decision-making, anomaly detection, personalization, intelligent automation, and predictive analytics across diverse industries.

Core Use Cases of AI in Messaging Workflows

1. **Anomaly Detection**
   Identify deviations from expected patterns in sensor data, transaction logs, or system telemetry.
2. **Predictive Routing**
   Route messages or requests dynamically based on predicted priority, resource availability, or user behavior.
3. **Personalization and Recommendation**
   Tailor event content or processing logic to individual users or sessions using trained models.
4. **Language Understanding and Classification**
   Use NLP to categorize, summarize, or escalate messages such as support requests or user feedback.
5. **Image, Audio, and Video Enrichment**
   Enrich media events in real time using cognitive services to extract metadata, transcribe speech, or detect objects.
6. **Autonomous Response and Remediation**
   Trigger automated corrective actions based on AI-driven assessments (e.g., scaling services, flagging fraud, blocking threats).

Integrating ML with Azure Messaging Services

Azure offers multiple pathways to embed ML models into message processing pipelines:

- **Inline inference** via Azure Functions calling Azure ML endpoints
- **Streaming analytics** with ML scoring using Azure Stream Analytics and ONNX models
- **Batch enrichment** of captured event streams using Synapse Pipelines or Databricks
- **On-device inference** using Azure IoT Edge and ML modules

Let's explore each of these approaches with examples and architecture patterns.

Inline Model Inference in Azure Functions

Azure Functions can act as intelligent message consumers. After receiving an event from Event Hubs or Service Bus, the function invokes a model endpoint deployed via Azure ML.

Example: Fraud Prediction

```
[FunctionName("PredictFraud")]

public async Task Run(

[EventHubTrigger("transactions", Connection = "EventHubConn")]
string[] events,
```

```
ILogger log)
{
foreach (var evt in events)
{
var transaction = JsonConvert.DeserializeObject<Transaction>(evt);
var prediction = await CallMLModel(transaction);
if (prediction.IsFraud)
{
await AlertTeam(transaction);
}
}
}
```

The CallMLModel method sends the transaction data to an Azure ML endpoint (real-time inference) and receives a score or classification.

This model could be trained on historical transaction features like amount, location, merchant, device fingerprint, etc.

Real-Time Scoring in Stream Analytics

Azure Stream Analytics supports real-time ML scoring using **ONNX** models. This is ideal for low-latency, high-volume use cases where inference needs to occur inline as events are processed.

Scenario: Predictive Maintenance in Manufacturing

```
SELECT
deviceId,
temperature,
pressure,
ML.Predict(maintenanceModel, temperature, pressure) AS failureRisk
INTO outputAlerts
FROM sensorInput
```

This query runs continuously and sends alerts when failureRisk exceeds a threshold.

Benefits:

- No outbound calls
- Low-latency scoring
- No extra hosting infrastructure

Batch Enrichment Using Synapse or Databricks

For captured events or historical data, batch processing pipelines are more suitable.

Architecture:

1. Event Hubs → Capture to Azure Data Lake

2. Synapse or Databricks reads events in batches
3. Applies ML models (PyTorch, SparkML, TensorFlow)
4. Outputs enriched events to Cosmos DB or SQL

Example: Video Platform Viewership Analysis

- Predict churn risk based on viewing patterns
- Cluster users based on behavior for A/B testing
- Recommend content categories using collaborative filtering

This approach allows the application of complex, multi-feature models on high volumes of stored data.

NLP and Cognitive Enrichment via Azure Cognitive Services

Azure Cognitive Services can be integrated to process text, audio, or images in real time.

Example: Support Ticket Classification via Event Grid

1. Event Grid receives a new support request
2. Azure Function triggered with message body
3. Function uses Text Analytics API:

```
var result = await client.AnalyzeSentimentAsync(ticket.Description);

var category = await client.ClassifyTextAsync(ticket.Description);
```

1. Routed to the correct team via custom logic

This enables triage and escalation to be handled automatically and intelligently.

Audio Events Example

- Voice telemetry from call center agents is transcribed using **Speech-to-Text**
- Sentiment is analyzed in real-time
- Routed differently based on emotional intensity or topic classification

---

Predictive Scaling and Auto-Remediation

ML can also optimize system operations.

Scenario: Auto-Scaling Consumers

Train a model that predicts load spikes in Event Hubs based on:

- Time of day
- Historical message rates
- Marketing campaigns

Use this prediction to scale Azure Function instances or Kubernetes consumer pods.

Scenario: Error Forecasting

Use past incidents to predict failure likelihood in specific topics or queues. Preemptively reroute or delay messages until the system stabilizes.

Tools and Services for ML Integration

Service	Purpose
Azure Machine Learning	Training, deploying, and managing ML models
Azure Cognitive Services	Ready-to-use AI APIs for vision, speech, language
Azure Synapse ML	Distributed training and inference in Synapse
Azure Data Explorer (ADX)	Time-series insights and lightweight ML scoring
ONNX Runtime	Lightweight inference engine for pre-trained models
ML.NET	Model training and scoring in .NET apps

Challenges and Best Practices

- **Latency Sensitivity**: Place models close to the event source or use compiled models (ONNX) for real-time use.
- **Security**: Ensure data passed to ML services is anonymized or encrypted, especially with PHI or financial data.
- **Explainability**: Consider integrating explainability frameworks (e.g., SHAP) to understand model decisions.

- **Monitoring**: Track model performance (e.g., accuracy, drift) alongside messaging metrics.
- **Versioning**: Maintain event schema versions and model versions together to avoid mismatches.

Real-World Use Case: AI-Driven Patient Monitoring

Organization: National Health Service Provider

Use Case:

- Stream real-time vitals from wearable devices via Event Hubs
- Use ML models to predict arrhythmias or cardiac arrest risk
- Send alerts to clinicians only when high-risk signals detected
- Automate triage and assign risk category via Logic Apps

Outcome:

- Reduced alarm fatigue
- 25% improvement in early intervention
- Automated compliance reporting

Summary

AI and ML are transforming how real-time systems operate. When integrated with Azure's robust messaging services, they enable systems to go beyond reactive event handling toward predictive, intelligent orchestration. From fraud detection and sentiment analysis to predictive maintenance and workload optimization, AI-driven messaging systems unlock immense value—provided they are implemented with care, governance, and scalability in mind.

The next section will focus on how to architect and prepare systems for the next generation of real-time, distributed applications, bringing together all emerging trends and best practices into future-ready solutions.

Preparing for the Next Generation of Event-Driven Architectures

As applications become increasingly distributed, intelligent, and responsive, event-driven architecture (EDA) continues to grow as the foundation of scalable, loosely coupled systems. The next generation of EDA will not only handle events but also interpret, transform, correlate, and act on them autonomously. To prepare for this future, organizations must design architectures that are modular, interoperable, cloud-native, observability-first, and enriched with contextual awareness through AI and analytics.

This section explores the strategic considerations, design patterns, tooling practices, and cultural shifts needed to prepare for the next generation of event-driven systems. It ties together messaging advancements, machine learning integration, open standards, and platform capabilities to guide architects and engineers in building resilient, future-ready infrastructures on Azure.

Rethinking Architecture: From Message Passing to Reactive Systems

Traditional event-based systems emphasize delivery guarantees—ensuring events are reliably passed from producer to consumer. Future systems must go further:

- **Contextual awareness**: Events should carry richer metadata for in-flight decisions.
- **Temporal reasoning**: Systems should correlate sequences, trends, and patterns over time.
- **Autonomous decisioning**: Consumers should not just process events but interpret them with logic or ML.

To support this, system design must evolve from mere pipelines into **reactive graphs** of interconnected services with well-defined flows, retries, filters, enrichments, and policies.

Architectural Foundations for Future-Ready Systems

1. Unified Event Fabric

Modern architectures should consolidate event routing into a central, policy-driven mesh. This enables uniform visibility, access control, auditing, and tracing.

- Use **Azure Event Grid Domains** for publisher-scoped routing
- Implement **Service Bus topics with filters** for fine-grained fan-out

- Overlay **Event Hubs as ingestion points** with multiple consumer groups
- Federate with **on-prem or third-party brokers** via Azure Relay or Hybrid Connections

Unified fabric makes governance, scale management, and platform observability more coherent.

2. Event-First Domain Modeling

Start with events as the source of truth. Each domain defines its:

- **Event contracts** (schema + metadata)
- **Event producers and owners**
- **Downstream consumers and responsibilities**

This aligns well with Domain-Driven Design (DDD) and decouples workflows.

Example:

```
{
"eventType": "PatientDischarged",
"version": "v1.2",
"data": {
"patientId": "p-1981",
"timestamp": "2025-05-09T16:00:00Z",
"location": "Ward A3",
```

"dischargedBy": "nurse-190"

}

}

Each event is immutable, traceable, and versioned.

Tooling and Platform Strategies

Schema Management

Implement **Azure Schema Registry** to:

- Avoid schema drift
- Provide contract-based development
- Automate validation at ingress

Integrate schema validation into CI/CD pipelines:

az schemaregistry schema register \

—name patientDischarged \

—schema-group clinicalEvents \

—definition @discharge-schema.avsc \

—format Avro

Distributed Tracing and Correlation

Use **OpenTelemetry** to track event lifecycle:

- Assign traceId, spanId, and correlationId to each event
- Propagate through Event Grid, Service Bus, Event Hubs
- Integrate with **Application Insights** or **Grafana Tempo**

This enables full system observability for performance and debugging.

Event Replay and Audit

Modern systems should support:

- Event replay from Event Hubs Capture or storage
- Reprocessing in dev/staging environments
- Governance around replay actions

Use cases include:

- Bug retroanalysis
- Retraining ML models
- Rebuilding state stores

Patterns for Composability and Modularity

To handle evolving requirements, architectures must be modular and composable.

Recommended Patterns:

- **Event Sourcing**: Use events to rebuild application state (especially with CQRS)
- **Outbox Pattern**: Ensure atomicity between database writes and event publication
- **Idempotent Consumers**: Consumers should tolerate retries without side effects
- **Circuit Breakers**: Prevent cascading failures from downstream issues
- **Replay Buffers**: Allow partial recovery and selective event reprocessing

These patterns reduce fragility and improve fault tolerance.

Enabling Dynamic Scaling and Adaptability

Adaptive Scaling

In the future, consumers and producers should scale reactively:

- Monitor IncomingMessages, ProcessingLatency
- Trigger scale-up/down via **Azure Kubernetes Events**, Functions' elastic plans
- Use **Event Hubs Auto-Inflate** for ingestion elasticity

Intelligent Load Shedding

As load increases, degrade gracefully:

- Drop non-critical events
- Delay low-priority batches
- Use Event Grid filters to suppress unneeded messages

Embracing AI in Event Workflows

Modern event-driven systems must be **intelligent by design**. Integrate AI to:

- Prioritize events dynamically
- Classify or route based on content
- Detect fraud, anomalies, or sentiment
- Auto-remediate when metrics indicate drift

Embed ML models in Azure Functions, call Azure ML endpoints, or use ASA with ONNX.

Governance and Compliance by Default

Future systems must enforce compliance and governance continuously:

- Encrypt all event data in transit and at rest (using CMK if needed)
- Log all access to event fabric

- Retain event logs as per data residency rules
- Implement **RBAC policies and Private Endpoints** for messaging services

Use **Azure Policy** to enforce deployment standards.

Developer Experience and Culture

Event-Driven Mindset

Encourage teams to:

- Define events in code and share across services
- Document expected consumers, retries, and fallbacks
- Write integration tests that simulate event flows

CI/CD for Events

- Validate schemas
- Enforce contract compatibility
- Test full message lifecycle in staging

Example GitHub Action:

```
- name: Validate Event Schema
run: |
schema-validator validate discharge-schema.avsc
```

Preparing the Organization

Preparing for the next generation is not just technical—it's cultural.

- **Create event product owners** for schemas and contracts
- **Build an internal event catalog** or discovery portal
- **Document SLAs** for latency, availability, and delivery
- **Share dashboards and incident reviews** across teams

This promotes shared ownership, transparency, and rapid iteration.

Summary

The next generation of event-driven architecture is already taking shape. By adopting modular, schema-first, intelligent, and observability-driven practices today, organizations can build messaging systems that are prepared for tomorrow's scale, complexity, and innovation. Azure's comprehensive ecosystem of messaging services, AI tooling, observability features, and governance frameworks equips architects and engineers with the tools needed to lead this transformation.

As we move into the final chapters of this book, we will reflect on the key takeaways and actionable steps for building resilient, scalable, and intelligent messaging platforms on Azure.

Chapter 11: Conclusion

Key Takeaways

As we bring this book to a close, it's important to reflect on the key principles, architectural practices, and strategic insights that have been shared throughout. Azure's comprehensive ecosystem for cloud messaging—comprising Azure Service Bus, Event Grid, and Event Hubs—empowers developers and architects to build systems that are scalable, responsive, and resilient. But building truly successful event-driven systems requires more than simply wiring up services; it demands careful planning, robust design patterns, security mindfulness, and a continuous improvement mindset.

This section distills the most crucial takeaways from each chapter and highlights how to apply them in real-world scenarios to maximize system reliability, efficiency, and maintainability.

Embrace the Evolution of Cloud Messaging

Cloud messaging has moved beyond traditional queues and brokers. Today's architectures must support real-time communication, event sourcing, stream analytics, and intelligent automation—all while adhering to enterprise security and compliance standards.

Key Insight: Messaging is no longer just a plumbing layer; it is an active, intelligent backbone that drives business-critical workflows.

Think in Events, Not Just Messages

Understanding the distinction between messaging and events is vital. Messages imply a directed command from a sender to a recipient. Events represent state changes that are broadcast, decoupling producers and consumers.

Design Recommendation:

- Use **Service Bus** for command-oriented workflows and ordered processing
- Use **Event Grid** for reactive event routing with minimal latency
- Use **Event Hubs** for telemetry ingestion and stream processing

---

Choose the Right Tool for the Job

Each Azure messaging service is purpose-built:

Scenario	Recommended Service
Distributed telemetry ingestion	Azure Event Hubs
Pub/Sub for app logic and automation	Azure Event Grid
Enterprise-grade message queuing	Azure Service Bus
Lightweight backend queues	Azure Storage Queues (basic)

Consider characteristics like ordering, dead-lettering, replay support, and throughput when making architectural decisions.

Design for Scale and Reliability

Architectures should be elastic, partition-tolerant, and modular. Embrace patterns like:

- **Event sourcing** for state management
- **CQRS** for decoupling read/write workloads
- **Outbox pattern** for transactional integrity
- **Dead-letter queues** for failure isolation

Implementation Tips:

- Use **auto-inflate** on Event Hubs
- Apply **prefetching** and **concurrent processing** for consumers
- Leverage **diagnostic settings** and **Azure Monitor** to track flow

---

Secure by Default

Security is a core consideration—not an afterthought.

Security Practices:

- Use **Managed Identities** instead of connection strings
- Enforce **RBAC** for least privilege
- Route traffic through **Private Endpoints**
- Encrypt data using **customer-managed keys (CMKs)**
- Monitor for **unauthorized access attempts** and **throttling anomalies**

Compliance is easier to maintain when security is built into the foundation.

Operate with Visibility

Observability enables proactive remediation and performance optimization.

Observability Best Practices:

- Set up **Azure Monitor alerts** for message backlog, throttling, and errors
- Enable **Log Analytics** for diagnostic querying and trend analysis
- Implement **distributed tracing** using correlationId propagation
- Track SLA compliance through **latency dashboards**

Having data is not enough—you must act on it continuously.

Automate and Iterate Continuously

Build pipelines that verify contracts, deploy artifacts, and run integration tests.

Automation Goals:

- Validate **event schema versions** before deployment
- Run **replay tests** using captured events
- Use **Infrastructure-as-Code (IaC)** to enforce consistency

- Implement **chaos testing** for consumers and message loss

Embrace a DevOps mindset across your messaging infrastructure.

Apply AI to Unlock Next-Level Capabilities

Intelligent event-driven systems use machine learning for:

- Fraud detection
- Customer personalization
- Predictive scaling
- Real-time sentiment analysis

Use Azure ML, Cognitive Services, and Stream Analytics to embed intelligence directly into event flows.

Example:

A Function processing transactions can invoke an Azure ML endpoint to classify high-risk activity and route it for manual review.

Prepare for What's Next

The future of event-driven systems includes:

- **Event Meshes**: Globally distributed, connected brokers
- **Schema registries** and **contract-first development**
- **Cross-cloud interoperability** using **CloudEvents**

- **Edge-driven event sourcing** for latency-sensitive domains

- **Self-healing systems** powered by autonomous analytics

Position your architecture now by adopting open standards, observability, and modularity.

Cultivate Organizational Maturity

Technology alone isn't enough. Success depends on cross-team alignment, documentation, governance, and continuous learning.

Organizational Best Practices:

- Appoint **event owners** for schema governance

- Maintain **an internal event catalog**

- Schedule **regular postmortems** on event-related incidents

- Offer **training and templates** to new teams

- Track and review **event-driven SLAs** (delivery, latency, fault tolerance)

Event-driven maturity should grow across architecture, operations, and culture.

Final Summary Table

Pillar	Actionable Step
Design	Model events as first-class citizens
Security	Use managed identities and private endpoints
Reliability	Leverage DLQs, retries, and idempotency
Observability	Track latency, throughput, and failure points
Intelligence	Integrate ML for routing and prediction
Governance	Enforce schema versioning and consumer contracts
Scaling	Design for elasticity and partitioned processing
Automation	Adopt CI/CD for infrastructure and event validation

Final Word

Event-driven systems are not just a technology trend—they are a strategic enabler of responsive, intelligent, and resilient applications. Azure provides the tools and platform maturity to help organizations build and evolve messaging systems that stand the test of time.

The remaining sections in this book offer additional appendices including reference guides, glossaries, and sample projects to reinforce practical implementation. Whether you are modernizing a legacy platform or launching a greenfield system, the principles laid out here will guide you toward successful outcomes in your real-time, cloud-native journey.

Next Steps for Deepening Expertise

While this book has provided a comprehensive foundation in Azure messaging and event-driven architecture, becoming a true expert in the field requires continued learning, hands-on practice, exploration of advanced scenarios, and staying up to date with the fast-evolving cloud ecosystem. Mastery comes from combining conceptual understanding with architectural insight, development discipline, operational rigor, and a mindset oriented around continuous improvement.

This section outlines structured and practical next steps to deepen your expertise in building and maintaining real-time cloud systems with Azure, covering areas such as advanced certifications, specialized patterns, performance tuning, cross-cloud interoperability, security hardening, and contributions to the broader cloud-native community.

Mastering the Azure Messaging Ecosystem

Begin by revisiting the core Azure messaging services—Service Bus, Event Grid, and Event Hubs—and mastering the advanced capabilities of each.

Recommended Hands-On Goals:

- Build multi-tier applications using **Service Bus sessions and dead-letter queues**
- Implement **Event Grid advanced filtering** and **retry policies**
- Use **Event Hubs Capture** to persist and reprocess telemetry data
- Create **high-throughput ingestion pipelines** with partition-aware producers

- Combine messaging with other services like Azure Functions, Logic Apps, Cosmos DB, and Synapse Analytics

By designing and deploying real-world scenarios that mimic production workloads, you will gain deeper insights into system behavior under varying conditions.

Explore Advanced Architectural Patterns

Once you're comfortable with basic integrations and deployments, push further into advanced architectural designs:

Deep-Dive Topics:

- **Event Sourcing and CQRS** with Service Bus and Azure SQL or Cosmos DB
- **Choreography vs. Orchestration** using Event Grid and Durable Functions
- **Saga patterns** to manage long-running, compensating workflows across services
- **Stream analytics and sliding windows** with Event Hubs + ASA
- **Resilient design** with retry backoff, poison message handling, and fallback logic

Create architecture diagrams for different business domains (e.g., logistics, banking, healthcare), and challenge yourself to apply appropriate messaging strategies to each.

Obtain Azure and Cloud Certifications

Certifications serve not only as formal validation of your skills but also provide structured learning paths.

Recommended Azure Certifications:

- **Azure Developer Associate (AZ-204)**
- **Azure Solutions Architect Expert (AZ-305)**
- **Azure Data Engineer Associate (DP-203)**
- **Azure AI Engineer Associate (AI-102)** for those exploring AI in event-driven systems

Supplement these with Kubernetes (CKA/CKAD) or CNCF certifications like **Certified Kubernetes Application Developer** for deeper orchestration knowledge.

Join the Event-Driven Development Community

Engage with the community to learn best practices, discover emerging trends, and stay informed of updates.

Where to Engage:

- **Microsoft Tech Community** and Azure blogs
- **GitHub** for open-source event-driven reference apps
- **Azure Architecture Center** and Patterns & Practices library

- **Stack Overflow and Reddit** for troubleshooting and ideation
- **Twitter/X** and LinkedIn to follow Azure engineers and architects
- **Cloud Native Computing Foundation** (CNCF) for vendor-neutral practices

Contribute by writing blog posts, sharing sample architectures, or giving lightning talks at meetups or webinars.

Automate, Observe, and Iterate

Build operational muscle by:

- Creating IaC templates for repeatable deployments (using **Terraform**, **Bicep**, or **ARM templates**)
- Implementing **end-to-end observability** with Application Insights, Log Analytics, and distributed tracing
- Setting up **CI/CD pipelines** that validate schemas, deploy infrastructure, and run integration tests

Create feedback loops that feed system telemetry into retrospectives, dashboards, and team performance reviews. Practice SRE (Site Reliability Engineering) principles such as error budgets, SLIs, and SLAs.

Prototype in Multi-Cloud and Hybrid Environments

Azure messaging services are excellent, but enterprise solutions often span hybrid or multi-cloud boundaries. Gain experience in:

- Bridging Azure Event Grid with AWS EventBridge or Google Pub/Sub
- Connecting on-prem brokers (e.g., RabbitMQ, Kafka, ActiveMQ) to Azure via Azure Relay or VPN
- Using **CloudEvents** for cross-cloud event format interoperability
- Setting up federated event mesh architectures using third-party tools like Solace or Confluent

This expertise is especially valuable in enterprise integration scenarios.

Experiment with Intelligent Workflows

Use real-world data to build intelligent, event-aware systems:

- Combine Event Hubs + Azure Stream Analytics + Azure ML for fraud or anomaly detection
- Build a chatbot that triggers via Event Grid on CRM ticket updates
- Create AI-powered recommendation engines driven by customer telemetry
- Incorporate cognitive enrichment (vision, speech, language) into media event pipelines

Train and deploy models using **Azure ML**, call them from Functions, and make them part of your messaging pipeline. Add validation and rollback logic for robustness.

Build Internal Playbooks and Templates

Become a center of excellence within your organization:

- Create internal starter kits for messaging-based apps
- Maintain documentation on approved event schemas and message contracts
- Develop troubleshooting guides, alerting templates, and failover runbooks
- Host architecture review sessions to guide teams adopting event-driven patterns

Evangelize consistency in how messaging systems are adopted and operated across your organization.

Track Emerging Technologies

Stay informed about:

- **Project Dapr**: For sidecar-based event-driven microservice design
- **CloudEvents + AsyncAPI**: For standardized event modeling and documentation
- **Edge messaging patterns** using Azure Stack Edge and IoT Edge
- **Serverless streaming** with containers, functions, and bindings

- **Zero-trust architecture** principles applied to message-level security

Set aside time each quarter to explore new services, SDK updates, or architectural patterns published by Microsoft and the wider community.

Create Your Own Reference Architecture

As a culminating exercise, design and document a complete system that includes:

- Multiple messaging services (e.g., Event Hubs + Service Bus + Event Grid)
- Consumer and producer services
- State stores and data platforms
- Observability, security, and resilience layers
- CI/CD, IaC, and schema governance

Host it on GitHub with documentation, runbooks, and sample data. Use it as both a learning platform and a reference point for future projects.

Summary

Becoming an expert in Azure messaging and event-driven architecture is not a linear journey—it's iterative, multidisciplinary, and collaborative. The best professionals combine architectural insight with operational discipline, development experience, and a passion for scalable, intelligent systems. By applying the next steps outlined here—through hands-on projects, certifications, community engagement, automation, and exploration—you will position yourself to lead in a future powered by real-time, intelligent, cloud-native architectures.

The final section of this book provides some closing thoughts and reflections to guide your long-term journey in the world of event-driven cloud design.

Final Thoughts

Event-driven architecture represents a profound shift in how systems are designed, built, and operated. It replaces rigid, request-based workflows with flexible, asynchronous, and decoupled interactions. It empowers systems to react in real time, scale gracefully under load, and remain resilient under failure. But more than just a technical paradigm, event-driven thinking transforms organizations—encouraging autonomy, enabling innovation, and fostering adaptability in a world that is increasingly defined by change.

This book has explored the full breadth of Azure's capabilities in building event-driven systems: from foundational concepts and service overviews to real-world case studies, AI integrations, and future-facing architecture strategies. As we close the final chapter, it's worth reflecting on the deeper implications of this architectural model—and what it means for you, your teams, and your applications going forward.

Embracing Events as the Language of Change

At the heart of event-driven systems is the idea that **events are the raw signals of change**. They are the atomic units of business activity—the "what happened" of your domain. When you embrace events as first-class citizens, you gain visibility into every meaningful action, decision, and outcome in your system.

This perspective enables a richer, more expressive way of modeling business processes. Instead of issuing imperative commands, systems become observers and reactors—capable of adapting to changing inputs without centralized orchestration.

Actionable Insight: Practice modeling your domain in terms of events. What are the key moments that matter? Who should know about them? What decisions or reactions should they trigger?

From Complexity to Composability

Event-driven architectures can appear complex at first glance: multiple services, asynchronous flows, retries, ordering, and monitoring challenges. But properly modularized, these systems are **composable**. Each producer and consumer is autonomous. Each piece of logic is independently deployable. Each failure is isolated and recoverable.

This composability pays enormous dividends as your system grows. It becomes easier to onboard new teams, evolve services, integrate partners, and experiment safely.

Best Practice: Design each event-driven component to be single-responsibility, independently testable, and infrastructure-agnostic. Focus on clarity, schema contracts, and graceful degradation.

Rethinking Time, State, and Causality

One of the most fundamental changes in event-driven systems is how we think about **time and state**. Events represent actions that occurred at a specific moment. Consumers reconstruct their understanding of the world by consuming these time-stamped facts.

State is no longer a monolithic database—it is **a projection derived from events**. This enables:

- Time travel (replay and audits)
- Parallel evolution of different views
- Robustness through immutability

Understanding **causality chains**—what led to what—becomes critical. This is why correlation IDs, distributed tracing, and event metadata are so important.

Guidance: Invest in tooling and practices that preserve event history, link causally related events, and enable flexible state reconstruction.

The Operational Shift: From Monitoring to Observability

Running event-driven systems in production demands a shift from traditional monitoring to **deep observability**. Because systems are decoupled, failures may not show up as 500 errors—they may appear as retries, delays, or eventual inconsistencies.

You need telemetry that tells a story: how an event flowed, how long it took to be processed, which services touched it, where it failed, and how it recovered.

This means:

- Implementing distributed tracing (OpenTelemetry, Application Insights)
- Logging structured data with trace and span context
- Monitoring KPIs like processing latency, backlog size, and failure rates
- Alerting on deviations from expected patterns—not just absolute thresholds

Recommendation: Define a minimum observability standard for all event-driven components, and enforce it as part of your CI/CD pipelines.

Change Management and Organizational Maturity

Technology doesn't succeed in isolation. The success of event-driven architecture depends on how your **teams, processes, and culture evolve** with it.

Key Organizational Capabilities:

- **Contract Ownership**: Teams are responsible for the events they publish—documenting schemas, setting expectations, and versioning responsibly.
- **Decentralized Governance**: Rather than a single architecture team owning all decisions, empower domain teams to manage their own messaging flows.
- **Operational Readiness**: Build runbooks, SLAs, health dashboards, and alerting for all services.

- **Continuous Learning**: Hold blameless postmortems. Share lessons learned across teams. Publish retrospectives.

Event-driven design fosters a **culture of autonomy with accountability**—one that scales with your engineering organization.

Looking Ahead: The Shape of What's to Come

As the cloud continues to evolve, so too will the event-driven paradigm. You can expect:

- **Greater standardization** (CloudEvents, AsyncAPI, OpenTelemetry)
- **Tighter integration** with AI/ML for adaptive systems
- **Advanced developer platforms** that generate scaffolding, simulate flows, and manage schema evolution
- **Distributed event mesh** architectures across regions, clouds, and edges
- **Streaming-native databases** that treat events as the canonical data store

To stay ahead, adopt a mindset of **curiosity, adaptability, and craftsmanship**. Make time to explore emerging tools. Contribute back through blog posts, demos, or talks. Mentor others entering the field.

Your Journey from Here

You've now developed a solid understanding of Azure's event-driven capabilities and how to apply them architecturally, operationally, and strategically. The next stage is yours to define.

You might:

- Modernize a legacy monolith into reactive services
- Launch a greenfield system that scales from day one
- Build developer platforms for others to consume messaging safely
- Automate an IoT fleet with edge event routing and ML insights
- Lead architecture reviews or operational excellence programs

Whatever the case, you are equipped to lead confidently—and to help your organization make the most of real-time, resilient, intelligent software systems.

Final Encouragement

The best systems are not the most complex—they are the most understandable, adaptable, and maintainable. The same is true of careers. Focus on fundamentals. Build for humans. Automate what's repetitive. Document what's nuanced. Test what's risky. Measure what matters. And above all, stay curious.

This book is complete—but your journey is just beginning.

Chapter 12: Appendices

Glossary of Terms

Understanding the foundational terminology of messaging and event-driven architecture is essential for clear communication, effective system design, and productive collaboration across development, operations, and business teams. This glossary compiles the essential terms used throughout this book and the broader Azure ecosystem, providing precise, concise definitions to serve as a lasting reference. These definitions are contextualized for Azure but generally applicable across cloud-native platforms and messaging paradigms.

A

ACK (Acknowledgment)

A confirmation sent by a message consumer to indicate successful processing. In Azure Service Bus, completion of a message via CompleteAsync() is an acknowledgment.

AMQP (Advanced Message Queuing Protocol)

An open standard application layer protocol for message-oriented middleware. Azure Service Bus and Event Hubs both support AMQP 1.0 for reliable, secure, and interoperable messaging.

AsyncAPI

An open standard for documenting asynchronous APIs, similar to how OpenAPI (Swagger) is used for synchronous REST APIs. Useful in event-driven architecture to define producers, consumers, and message contracts.

B

Backoff Strategy

A retry mechanism that gradually increases the delay between successive attempts, often used with exponential growth to handle transient faults.

Blob Storage

An Azure storage service used for storing large amounts of unstructured data. Often used with Event Hubs Capture to persist event streams.

C

Capture (Event Hubs Capture)

A feature of Azure Event Hubs that automatically writes incoming events to Azure Blob Storage or Data Lake in Avro format for batch processing, archiving, or replay.

Consumer Group

A named view of an Event Hub, allowing multiple independent readers to consume the same event stream at their own pace. Each consumer group has its own set of offsets.

Correlation ID

A unique identifier shared across related events, requests, or processes, enabling distributed tracing and event flow reconstruction.

CQRS (Command Query Responsibility Segregation)

A pattern that separates read and write operations into different models, often used alongside event sourcing to optimize scalability and performance.

D

Dead-Letter Queue (DLQ)

A secondary queue used to isolate messages that cannot be delivered or processed due to issues like schema mismatches, delivery retries exhaustion, or validation failures.

Durable Functions

An extension of Azure Functions for writing stateful orchestrations in a serverless fashion. Often used to implement sagas or workflows in event-driven applications.

E

EDA (Event-Driven Architecture)

A design paradigm where systems communicate by producing and reacting to events. It decouples producers and consumers, allowing for more flexible, scalable, and resilient systems.

Event Grid

An Azure service for building reactive, publish-subscribe eventing systems with near real-time latency and support for custom topics and domains.

Event Hubs

A high-throughput, big data event ingestion service in Azure. Used for streaming telemetry, log data, and time-series data.

Event Sourcing

A pattern where application state is built from a sequence of immutable events, rather than storing only the latest state snapshot.

F

Fan-Out / Fan-In

Fan-out refers to broadcasting events to multiple subscribers. Fan-in refers to consolidating multiple event sources into a single stream or handler.

FIFO (First-In, First-Out)

A message delivery order guaranteeing that the first message sent is the first to be received. Azure Service Bus supports FIFO using message sessions.

G

Geo-DR (Geo-Disaster Recovery)

A feature that replicates Azure Service Bus or Event Hubs namespaces across regions for business continuity in case of regional failures.

H

Hybrid Connections

A service used to securely connect Azure services with on-premises systems over outbound TCP connections. Frequently used for integrating legacy message brokers or databases.

I

Idempotency

The property of an operation to have the same effect no matter how many times it is performed. Critical for ensuring safe retries in event processing.

Ingress

The entry point for data into a messaging system, such as an Event Hub producer client sending telemetry.

K

Kafka (Apache Kafka)

A distributed streaming platform. Azure Event Hubs is compatible with Kafka protocols, allowing Kafka clients to write to Event Hubs without change.

KQL (Kusto Query Language)

The query language used in Azure Log Analytics and Azure Data Explorer, commonly used for querying telemetry, logs, and metrics in messaging systems.

L

Latency

The time taken for a message to travel from producer to consumer. Important performance metric in real-time messaging.

Logic Apps

A low-code/no-code Azure service for orchestrating workflows. Often used for event-based automation and integration with SaaS platforms.

M

Message Session

A feature in Azure Service Bus to group related messages for ordered processing. Enables FIFO processing within a session.

Managed Identity

An Azure identity used for authenticating services without managing credentials. Enables secure access to Service Bus, Event Hubs, and Event Grid.

Message Lock

A temporary hold on a message after it's dequeued from a queue, preventing others from processing it until it's completed or abandoned.

O

Offset

A pointer to the position of an event in an Event Hub partition. Used by consumers to track progress.

OpenTelemetry

An open standard for observability, providing APIs and SDKs for metrics, logs, and tracing. Supported by Azure Monitor for distributed systems.

P

Partition

A unit of parallelism and scalability in Event Hubs. Events are distributed across partitions for concurrent processing.

Poison Message

A message that causes repeated failures in consumers, often ending up in the DLQ after exceeding retry attempts.

Producer

A component or system that generates and sends events or messages into a messaging system.

Q

Queue

A data structure or messaging service that stores messages until they are processed. Azure offers Service Bus Queues and Storage Queues.

R

Retry Policy

A mechanism for reattempting message processing after failure. Supports backoff strategies and transient fault tolerance.

Replay

The process of reprocessing historical events, often from Event Hubs Capture or DLQ, to rebuild state or simulate scenarios.

S

Schema Registry

A centralized repository for storing, validating, and evolving event schemas. Azure offers a schema registry for Event Hubs and Kafka.

Service Bus

A fully managed enterprise messaging service for decoupling applications and services. Supports queues, topics, sessions, and DLQs.

Stream Analytics (ASA)

A real-time data stream processing service used to analyze and act on data from Event Hubs, IoT Hub, and other sources.

T

Throughput Unit (TU)

A capacity unit in Event Hubs that defines the ingress/egress limits. Can be scaled up or auto-inflated.

Topic

A Service Bus entity that supports publish-subscribe patterns, allowing messages to be filtered and routed to multiple subscribers.

V

VNet Integration

The ability to connect Azure services to a virtual network for improved security and access control.

W

Watermark

A concept in stream processing representing the event time up to which all events have been received. Useful in out-of-order stream analytics.

Z

Zero Trust

A security principle where no entity is trusted by default. Applied to messaging by enforcing identity validation, minimal access, and encrypted channels.

Summary

This glossary offers a foundational lexicon for navigating the world of Azure messaging and event-driven systems. Whether you're designing solutions, writing code, or operating infrastructure, familiarity with these terms will sharpen your communication, improve your documentation, and ensure that architectural decisions are grounded in a shared understanding of core concepts. As the ecosystem continues to evolve, revisit and expand this glossary to reflect new patterns, services, and innovations in the real-time cloud-native space.

Resources for Further Learning

Mastery in messaging systems and event-driven architecture requires more than theoretical knowledge—it demands ongoing exploration, experimentation, and engagement with evolving tools, communities, and thought leadership. Azure's ecosystem is rich with documentation, sample projects, videos, learning platforms, and community contributions that offer deeper understanding and practical expertise. Whether you're a developer, architect, or platform engineer, having a curated set of learning resources is critical to maintaining currency and growing in proficiency.

This section compiles and categorizes the most valuable learning resources, platforms, and strategies to support your continued journey into Azure messaging and event-driven systems.

Official Azure Documentation

Microsoft maintains extensive documentation for every service and feature in its messaging stack. These resources are always up to date and written with practical examples and CLI/SDK usage.

Key Portals:

- **Azure Service Bus**

  https://learn.microsoft.com/azure/service-bus-messaging/

- **Azure Event Grid**

  https://learn.microsoft.com/azure/event-grid/

- **Azure Event Hubs**

  https://learn.microsoft.com/azure/event-hubs/

- **Azure Stream Analytics**

  https://learn.microsoft.com/azure/stream-analytics/

- **Azure Schema Registry**

https://learn.microsoft.com/azure/event-hubs/schema-registry-overview

Each of these documentation portals includes quickstarts, how-to guides, REST APIs, SDK samples, and best practices.

Learning Paths and Tutorials

Microsoft Learn is a powerful, interactive platform that combines guided learning with sandboxed environments for experimentation.

Recommended Learning Paths:

1. **Implement messaging in Azure**
   https://learn.microsoft.com/training/paths/implement-message-based-communication/ [1]
2. **Design and implement event-driven architectures**
   https://learn.microsoft.com/training/modules/design-event-driven-architecture/ [2]
3. **Explore Azure messaging services**
   https://learn.microsoft.com/training/modules/choose-messaging-model/ [3]
4. **Azure architecture patterns**
   https://learn.microsoft.com/azure/architecture/patterns/ [4]

---

1. https://learn.microsoft.com/training/paths/implement-message-based-communication/
2. https://learn.microsoft.com/training/modules/design-event-driven-architecture/
3. https://learn.microsoft.com/training/modules/choose-messaging-model/
4. https://learn.microsoft.com/azure/architecture/patterns/

Each module includes hands-on labs, quizzes, and scenario-based challenges to reinforce concepts.

Books and eBooks

Reading published works by cloud architects and engineers can provide deeper strategic insights.

Notable Titles:

- *Designing Event-Driven Systems* by Ben Stopford

  (O'Reilly Media – Kafka and event-first thinking, applicable to Azure Event Hubs)

- *Cloud Native Patterns* by Cornelia Davis

  (Includes messaging and eventing in distributed systems)

- *Microsoft Azure Architecture Best Practices*

  (Microsoft Press – for broader platform alignment)

- *The Art of Scalability* by Abbott & Fisher

  (Cross-architecture techniques relevant to messaging scale strategies)

GitHub Repositories and Sample Projects

Microsoft and its community maintain numerous public repositories showcasing production-grade implementations and integrations.

Microsoft Samples:

- **azure-quickstart-templates**

  https://github.com/Azure/azure-quickstart-templates

  (Search: servicebus, eventhubs, eventgrid)

- **azure-event-grid-viewer**

  https://github.com/Azure-Samples/azure-event-grid-viewer

  (Real-time event visualization using Event Grid)

- **event-driven-architecture-reference**

  https://github.com/Azure-Samples/event-driven-architecture-reference

  (End-to-end example with Bicep, Functions, Event Grid, and Service Bus)

- **azure-messaging-samples**

  https://github.com/Azure/azure-sdk-for-net/tree/main/sdk/servicebus/Azure.Messaging.ServiceBus/samples

Cloning and running these samples is a fast track to understanding real-world integration challenges.

Blogs and Expert Articles

Consuming long-form content and architectural case studies accelerates pattern recognition and cross-domain thinking.

Must-Read Sources:

- **Azure Architecture Center Blog**

  https://techcommunity.microsoft.com/t5/azure-architecture-blog/bg-p/AzureArchitecture

- **Microsoft Tech Community**

  https://techcommunity.microsoft.com/

- **Mark Heath's Blog**

  https://markheath.net[5]

  (Excellent Azure Functions and messaging patterns)

- **Azure Friday (video blog)**

  https://azure.microsoft.com/resources/videos/azure-friday/

Online Courses and Certifications

For structured, instructor-led learning and certification preparation:

Platforms:

- **Pluralsight** – Courses on Azure messaging, architecture, event-driven patterns
- **LinkedIn Learning** – Azure Fundamentals to Expert-level certification prep

5. https://markheath.net/

- **Coursera / edX** – Microsoft-sponsored Azure courses
- **A Cloud Guru** – DevOps and advanced Azure concepts

Certifications:

- **AZ-204** – Developing Solutions for Microsoft Azure
- **AZ-305** – Designing Microsoft Azure Infrastructure Solutions
- **DP-203** – Data Engineering on Microsoft Azure (for streaming & analytics)

Tools and Emulators

Hands-on experimentation is a key part of developing fluency in messaging systems.

Useful Tools:

- **Service Bus Explorer (open source)**

https://github.com/paolosalvatori/ServiceBusExplorer

(Desktop tool for managing queues, topics, DLQs)

- **Event Grid Viewer (live demo)**

https://eventgridviewer.azurewebsites.net/

- **Azure Storage Explorer**

https://azure.microsoft.com/features/storage-explorer/

(Inspect and manage blob containers, useful for Event Hubs Capture)

- **Postman Collections for Event Grid / Service Bus APIs**

For testing REST endpoints directly.

Community Engagement

Learning from peers and contributors broadens your perspective and exposes you to non-trivial use cases.

Communities to Join:

- **Azure Developer Discord**

(https://aka.ms/azuredevdiscord)

- **Stack Overflow** (Tags: azure-servicebus, azure-eventgrid, azure-eventhubs)

- **Reddit** – r/AZURE

- **CNCF Slack** – Channels for CloudEvents, AsyncAPI, OpenTelemetry

Attend virtual meetups, Azure bootcamps, and webinars regularly.

Practice Projects to Build

Apply what you've learned by creating small, scoped projects that mirror real-world complexity:

1. **Real-time Order Processing System**

○ Use Event Grid for order placement notifications

○ Service Bus for orchestrating payment, inventory, and shipping

○ Azure Functions for micro-logics

2. **IoT Sensor Dashboard**

○ Ingest telemetry via Event Hubs

○ Process with Azure Stream Analytics

○ Visualize using Power BI or Grafana

3. **Intelligent Support System**

○ Event Grid triggers on new support tickets

○ Use Azure Cognitive Services to classify and summarize

○ Route to Service Bus queues per team

4. **DLQ Management Tool**

○ Read DLQs from Service Bus

○ Expose an admin UI for review/replay

○ Integrate with GitHub for audit trail

Summary

Continuous learning is not optional in the fast-moving world of cloud-native architecture. This curated set of resources—ranging from hands-on tutorials and documentation to advanced books and community engagement—is designed to accelerate your path toward mastery in Azure messaging and event-driven systems.

Return to these sources frequently. Subscribe to newsletters. Follow experts. Build and share. Most importantly, stay curious and make learning a habit. This ecosystem rewards those who explore it deeply, experiment boldly, and contribute generously.

Sample Projects and Code Snippets

While architectural understanding and theoretical knowledge provide the foundation for event-driven development, hands-on practice is the most effective way to internalize and master Azure's messaging ecosystem. Sample projects and code snippets allow you to explore design patterns, debug real-world workflows, and develop the intuition necessary to troubleshoot, optimize, and evolve production systems.

This section presents detailed, practical examples and reusable code segments that demonstrate key features of Azure Service Bus, Event Grid, and Event Hubs. These include project ideas, end-to-end use case implementations, and integration snippets using various Azure SDKs, serverless functions, and automation tools.

Project 1: Real-Time Order Processing System

Overview: Simulates an e-commerce system with loosely coupled services for order submission, payment, inventory, and shipping using Azure messaging services.

Architecture Components:

- **Event Grid Topic** → Receives order placed events
- **Azure Functions** → Subscribed to Event Grid for orchestrating
- **Service Bus Topics** → Used to route to payment and inventory services
- **Azure Table Storage** → Used for persisting order state
- **Logic App** → Sends email confirmations after shipping

Sample: Publishing to Event Grid from a Web API

```
var topicEndpoint = new Uri("https://my-topic.westus2-1.eventgrid.azure.net/api/events");

var topicKey = "your-topic-key";

var client = new EventGridPublisherClient(topicEndpoint, new AzureKeyCredential(topicKey));

var events = new List<EventGridEvent>

{

new EventGridEvent(
```

```
subject: "order/created",
eventType: "OrderCreated",
dataVersion: "1.0",
data: new
{
orderId = "ORD-1224",
customerId = "CUST-011",
totalAmount = 349.99
})
};
await client.SendEventsAsync(events);
```

Project 2: IoT Telemetry Ingestion and Alerting

Overview: Ingests temperature and humidity data from simulated IoT devices and triggers alerts when thresholds are breached.

Components:

- **Azure Event Hubs** → For ingesting telemetry at scale
- **Azure Stream Analytics** → For filtering and aggregation
- **Azure Functions** → For acting on alerts
- **Event Grid** → Publishes anomaly notifications

- **Power BI / Grafana** → Dashboard for real-time monitoring

Sample: ASA Query for Alert Detection

```
SELECT
deviceId,
AVG(temperature) AS avgTemp
INTO
alertOutput
FROM
telemetryInput TIMESTAMP BY enqueuedTime
GROUP BY
TumblingWindow(minute, 1),
deviceId
HAVING
AVG(temperature) > 80
```

Project 3: Customer Support Workflow with Dead-Letter Handling

Overview: Builds a support ticket system using queues with logic for retries, DLQ routing, and replaying failed messages.

Components:

- **Service Bus Queue** → Incoming support tickets
- **Azure Function** → Processes tickets with simulated errors
- **DLQ Monitor (Timer Triggered Function)** → Reads DLQs, logs, and optionally reprocesses
- **Cosmos DB** → Persists ticket metadata

Sample: Handling Messages in Azure Function

```
[FunctionName("ProcessSupportTicket")]

public async Task Run(

[ServiceBusTrigger("tickets", Connection = "ServiceBusConnection")] ServiceBusReceivedMessage message,

ServiceBusMessageActions messageActions,

ILogger log)

{

try

{

var ticket = JsonSerializer.Deserialize<Ticket>(message.Body);

log.LogInformation($"Processing ticket: {ticket.Id}");

// Simulate random failure
```

```
if (ticket.Priority == "High" && new Random().Next(0, 3) == 0)

{

throw new Exception("Simulated processing failure.");

}

await messageActions.CompleteMessageAsync(message);

}

catch (Exception ex)

{

log.LogError($"Error: {ex.Message}. Sending to DLQ.");

await messageActions.DeadLetterMessageAsync(message, "ProcessingError", ex.Message);

}

}
```

Project 4: Serverless Event Mesh for Microservices

Overview: Microservices communicate using Event Grid and Service Bus, with topic-based routing, filtering, and event enrichment.

Components:

- **Event Grid Domain** → Routes events per microservice publisher
- **Custom Topics** → Subscribed by internal services

- **Filters** → Limit subscriptions to relevant event types
- **Azure API Management** → Gateway for publishing externally

Sample: Creating a Filtered Event Subscription via CLI

```
az eventgrid event-subscription create \

—name process-invoice-sub \

—source-resource-id
"/subscriptions/<sub>/resourceGroups/<rg>/providers/
Microsoft.EventGrid/topics/invoice-topic" \

—endpoint https://my-function.azurewebsites.net/runtime/
webhooks/eventgrid \

—included-event-types "InvoiceCreated" \

—subject-begins-with "/finance/invoices/" \

—deadletter-storage-account-id
"/subscriptions/<sub>/resourceGroups/<rg>/providers/
Microsoft.Storage/storageAccounts/dlqstorage"
```

Project 5: Cross-Service Audit Trail System

Overview: Tracks a correlation ID across various Azure services including Event Grid, Service Bus, and Function Apps to build an auditable timeline of user activity.

Strategy:

- Generate correlationId at the frontend or initial producer
- Pass via custom headers or event metadata
- Propagate through all downstream messages and logs
- Query Application Insights using KQL to trace lifecycle

Sample: Logging Correlation ID in Function App

```
[FunctionName("TrackActivity")]

public void Run(

[EventGridTrigger] EventGridEvent eventGridEvent,

ILogger log)

{

var correlationId = eventGridEvent.Subject.Contains("correlationId")

? eventGridEvent.Subject.Split("/")[^1]

: Guid.NewGuid().ToString();

log.LogInformation($"[Correlation: {correlationId}] Processing event: {eventGridEvent.EventType}");

}
```

Best Practices Demonstrated

Each of the above projects reinforces core practices:

- **Idempotency**: Ensure handlers are safe to run multiple times
- **Schema Validation**: Use shared data contracts, validate input
- **Resilience**: Implement retries, DLQs, fallback mechanisms
- **Observability**: Trace events, log with context, measure KPIs
- **Security**: Use Managed Identity, least-privilege, and encryption
- **Versioning**: Support versioned schemas for evolution

Sample Utility Scripts

Use these snippets in your day-to-day workflow.

Export Messages from DLQ

```
az servicebus message peek \
—namespace-name myns \
—queue-name myqueue/$DeadLetterQueue \
—max-message-count 10 \
```

—output json

Restart Consumer on Message Threshold

```
az monitor metrics alert create \
—name restart-consumer \
—condition "avg ActiveMessages > 1000" \
—action-group restart-actions \
—description "Consumer lag detected"
```

Summary

Sample projects and code snippets act as launchpads for real-world implementation. Whether you're building a transactional queueing system, a high-volume telemetry pipeline, or a microservices messaging mesh, the examples here offer scaffolding, patterns, and tactical guidance for robust, testable, and scalable solutions. Clone them, adapt them, extend them—and most importantly, use them to learn by doing.

API Reference Guide

A clear understanding of the APIs that underpin Azure's messaging services is essential for both developers building event-driven solutions and operations teams supporting them. Whether you're working with Azure Service Bus for reliable messaging, Event Hubs for high-throughput telemetry, or Event Grid for event routing, knowing how to interact with these services programmatically allows for greater automation, observability, and integration flexibility.

This section serves as a reference guide to key Azure messaging service APIs—focusing on SDK usage patterns, REST endpoints, authentication methods, and operational tasks. It provides representative examples for common tasks across multiple languages and platforms, as well as guidance on secure access and performance best practices.

Azure Service Bus API Reference

Azure Service Bus supports both REST and SDK-based interactions. For most development, the Azure SDKs offer a cleaner, more intuitive abstraction over raw REST APIs.

SDK References:

- .NET: Azure.Messaging.ServiceBus
- Python: azure-servicebus
- JavaScript: @azure/service-bus
- Java: com.azure:azure-messaging-servicebus

Common Use Cases

Send a Message (C#)

```
var client = new ServiceBusClient(connectionString);

var sender = client.CreateSender("orders");

var message = new ServiceBusMessage("{ \"orderId\": \"1234\" }")

{
```

```
ContentType = "application/json",
CorrelationId = "corr-001",
TimeToLive = TimeSpan.FromMinutes(30)
};
await sender.SendMessageAsync(message);
```

Receive a Message (Node.js)

```
const { ServiceBusClient } = require("@azure/service-bus");
const sbClient = new ServiceBusClient(connectionString);
const receiver = sbClient.createReceiver("orders", { receiveMode: "peekLock" });
receiver.subscribe({
processMessage: async (message) => {
console.log(`Received: ${message.body}`);
await receiver.completeMessage(message);
},
processError: async (error) => {
console.error(error);
}
});
```

REST API Endpoint

```
POST
https://{namespace}.servicebus.windows.net/{queue}/messages

Authorization: SharedAccessSignature
sr=...&sig=...&se=...&skn=...

Content-Type: application/json
```

Azure Event Hubs API Reference

Event Hubs supports Apache Kafka APIs, AMQP 1.0, and HTTP-based ingestion, but most production usage leverages the SDKs for efficient, parallelized ingestion and consumption.

SDK References:

- .NET: Azure.Messaging.EventHubs
- Python: azure-eventhub
- JavaScript: @azure/event-hubs
- Java: com.azure:azure-messaging-eventhubs

Common Use Cases

Send Events (Python)

```
from azure.eventhub import EventHubProducerClient, EventData

producer =
EventHubProducerClient.from_connection_string(conn_str,
eventhub_name="telemetry")

event_data_batch = producer.create_batch()
```

```
event_data_batch.add(EventData('{"temperature": 72, "device": "sensor-1"}'))

producer.send_batch(event_data_batch)

producer.close()
```

Receive Events (Java)

```
EventHubConsumerAsyncClient consumer = new EventHubClientBuilder()

.consumerGroup(EventHubClientBuilder.DEFAULT_CONSUMER_GR

.connectionString(connectionString, eventHubName)

.buildAsyncConsumerClient();

consumer.receive(false)

.subscribe(partitionEvent -> {

System.out.println("Received event: " + partitionEvent.getData().getBodyAsString());

});
```

REST API Ingestion (Basic Example)

```
POST https://{namespace}.servicebus.windows.net/{eventhub}/messages

Authorization: SharedAccessSignature ...

Content-Type: application/json
```

Note: REST ingestion is throttled and limited—SDK or AMQP is preferred for production use.

Azure Event Grid API Reference

Event Grid uses HTTPS/REST for all operations, including event publishing, subscription management, and domain configuration.

SDK References:

- .NET: Azure.Messaging.EventGrid
- Python: azure-eventgrid
- JavaScript: @azure/eventgrid
- Java: com.azure:azure-messaging-eventgrid

Event Publishing (C#)

```
var client = new EventGridPublisherClient(
new Uri("https://mytopic.region-1.eventgrid.azure.net/api/events"),
new AzureKeyCredential("your-topic-key"));
await client.SendEventAsync(new EventGridEvent(
subject: "new-user",
eventType: "UserRegistered",
dataVersion: "1.0",
data: new { userId = "123", email = "test@example.com" }));
```

REST API for Subscriptions

Create Event Subscription

PUT https://management.azure.com/subscriptions/{subId}/resourceGroups/{rg}/providers/Microsoft.EventGrid/topics/{topic}/eventSubscriptions/{subscriptionName}?api-version=2022

Content-Type: application/json

Authorization: Bearer <token>

Payload:

```
{
"properties": {
"destination": {
"endpointType": "WebHook",
"properties": {
"endpointUrl": "https://myapp.azurewebsites.net/webhook"
}
},
"filter": {
"includedEventTypes": ["OrderPlaced"],
"subjectBeginsWith": "/orders/"
}
```

}

}

Authentication and Security

Azure supports multiple authentication models for messaging services:

- **Shared Access Signatures (SAS)**: Used for tokens with limited time and scope.
- **Managed Identity (MSI)**: Best practice for internal Azure services.
- **Azure AD OAuth**: Preferred for role-based access, automation, and cross-service security.

Example: Using Managed Identity in Azure Function (Service Bus)

```
var client = new ServiceBusClient("<fully-qualified-namespace>.servicebus.windows.net", new DefaultAzureCredential());
```

Ensure the managed identity has Azure Service Bus Data Sender or Receiver roles assigned.

Monitoring and Operations APIs

Azure provides management and operational APIs via Azure Monitor, Resource Graph, and ARM templates.

Query Message Metrics via Azure Monitor REST

GET https://management.azure.com/subscriptions/{subId}/resourceGroups/{rg}/providers/Microsoft.ServiceBus/namespaces/{ns}/queues/{queue}/providers/microsoft.insights/metrics?metricnames=ActiveMessages&api-version=2018-01-01

Authorization: Bearer <token>

ARM Template Snippet for Queue with DLQ

```
{
"type": "Microsoft.ServiceBus/namespaces/queues",
"name": "[parameters('queueName')]",
"apiVersion": "2022-10-01-preview",
"properties": {
"enablePartitioning": false,
"requiresDuplicateDetection": true,
"deadLetteringOnMessageExpiration": true,
"maxDeliveryCount": 10
}
}
```

Cross-Service Automation

Azure CLI, Bicep, Terraform, and PowerShell allow automation of messaging infrastructure.

Azure CLI: Create Event Grid Topic and Subscription

az eventgrid topic create—name orders-topic—resource-group messaging-rg—location westus2

az eventgrid event-subscription create \

—name notify-user \

—source-resource-id /subscriptions/<id>/resourceGroups/messaging-rg/providers/Microsoft.EventGrid/topics/orders-topic \

—endpoint https://myfunction.azurewebsites.net/runtime/webhooks/eventgrid

Terraform Example: Azure Service Bus Queue

resource "azurerm_servicebus_namespace" "example" {

name = "example-sbns"

location = azurerm_resource_group.example.location

resource_group_name = azurerm_resource_group.example.name

sku = "Standard"

}

resource "azurerm_servicebus_queue" "example" {

name = "orders"

```
namespace_id = azurerm_servicebus_namespace.example.id
max_delivery_count = 10
enable_partitioning = false
}
```

Summary

This API Reference Guide provides the foundational blocks for programmatically interacting with Azure messaging services. Whether sending events, managing queues, or subscribing to topics, developers can confidently build, automate, and secure their messaging infrastructure using SDKs and REST interfaces. As systems grow in complexity, leveraging these APIs for observability, resilience, and compliance will be essential to maintaining operational excellence. Always consult the official API versions and SDK changelogs to stay aligned with the latest capabilities and practices.

Frequently Asked Questions

This section compiles the most common and critical questions developers, architects, and operations teams encounter when working with Azure messaging services and event-driven architectures. These FAQs address real-world challenges ranging from configuration and scaling to security, performance, monitoring, and system integration.

By providing detailed explanations and actionable answers, this section serves as a quick-access troubleshooting and planning companion for anyone designing or maintaining messaging systems in Azure.

What's the difference between Azure Service Bus, Event Grid, and Event Hubs?

- **Service Bus** is best for high-reliability messaging (queues and topics), ordered delivery, transactions, and workflow control.

- **Event Grid** is optimized for lightweight event routing, reactive programming, and integration with Azure services.

- **Event Hubs** is used for telemetry ingestion and streaming large volumes of data from IoT devices, apps, and services.

Summary:

- Use **Service Bus** for transactional enterprise messaging.

- Use **Event Grid** for real-time event notification and serverless triggers.

- Use **Event Hubs** for streaming data at high scale.

When should I use a topic instead of a queue in Azure Service Bus?

Use a **topic** when multiple consumers need to receive the same message. Each consumer subscribes to the topic and receives a copy of the message.

Use a **queue** when a single consumer should process the message, and you want to use load balancing or point-to-point communication.

How do I ensure message ordering in Service Bus?

Enable **sessions** on the queue or topic. When you send messages with the same SessionId, they will be processed in order by a single consumer. The client must also use a **session-enabled receiver**.

```
var sender = client.CreateSender("orders");

await sender.SendMessageAsync(new ServiceBusMessage("msg1") { SessionId = "user123" });

var receiver = client.AcceptSessionAsync("orders", "user123");
```

How can I retry failed messages automatically?

In Azure Service Bus, messages that fail to be completed after MaxDeliveryCount are moved to the **Dead-Letter Queue (DLQ)**.

Best practice:

- Use **PeekLock** mode for processing
- Implement logic to CompleteMessageAsync() on success, or AbandonMessageAsync() on transient errors
- Monitor DLQs and use scheduled replay mechanisms

How can I access messages in the Dead-Letter Queue?

DLQs are accessed using a special path:

```
var receiver = client.CreateReceiver("myqueue", new ServiceBusReceiverOptions {

SubQueue = SubQueue.DeadLetter
```

});

You can also access via Azure CLI:

```
az servicebus topic subscription show \
—resource-group myrg \
—namespace-name myns \
—topic-name mytopic \
—name sub1 \
—query "countDetails.deadLetterMessageCount"
```

What's the maximum message size?

- **Service Bus**:
  - Standard: 256 KB
  - Premium: 1 MB
- **Event Hubs**:
  - Up to 1 MB per event
- **Event Grid**:
  - 1 MB per event in advanced tiers (64 KB default)

For large payloads, store data in **Blob Storage** and send a reference in the message.

Can I publish to Event Grid from outside Azure?

Yes. Use a **custom topic** and generate a **shared access key**. You can then send events over HTTPS using REST or any SDK.

POST https://<topic-name>.<region>-1.eventgrid.azure.net/api/events

Content-Type: application/json

aeg-sas-key: <your-topic-key>

How do I scale message consumers?

For **Azure Functions**, use **event-driven triggers** (Event Hub, Service Bus, Event Grid) that scale automatically with consumption plans or Premium Functions.

For custom apps:

- Partition consumers by message key or session ID
- Use Event Hub's consumer groups
- Scale out Kubernetes deployments with HorizontalPodAutoscaler
- Monitor ActiveMessages and IncomingRequests for scaling signals

---

How can I trace an event end-to-end?

Use a **correlation ID** embedded in every event:

1. Add correlationId property when publishing

2. Log the ID in every consumer/handler
3. Use **Application Insights** or **OpenTelemetry** to connect logs and metrics

```
message.ApplicationProperties["correlationId"] = context.TraceIdentifier;

traces

| where customDimensions.correlationId == "abc-123"
```

Is Event Hubs compatible with Kafka?

Yes. Azure Event Hubs provides **Kafka endpoint compatibility**, allowing Kafka clients to connect directly without changes to your application code.

Configure producer/consumer clients with:

```
bootstrap.servers=<eventhubs-namespace>.servicebus.windows.net:9093

security.protocol=SASL_SSL

sasl.mechanism=PLAIN
```

Use **Azure AD** or **SAS token** authentication.

How do I monitor and alert on message queues?

Use **Azure Monitor** to set up alerts on metrics such as:

- ActiveMessages
- DeadLetterMessageCount
- IncomingMessages

- ThrottledRequests
- DeliveryFailures (Event Grid)

Example CLI alert:

az monitor metrics alert create \

—name "HighQueueDepth" \

—resource "/subscriptions/xxx/resourceGroups/rg/providers/Microsoft.ServiceBus/namespaces/ns/queues/myqueue" \

—condition "avg ActiveMessages > 500"

Can Event Grid guarantee delivery?

Event Grid uses **at-least-once delivery**. It guarantees delivery to all subscribers, retrying for up to 24 hours using exponential backoff.

To handle duplicate events:

- Make event handlers **idempotent**
- Track event.id or your own deduplication key

What's the best practice for schema evolution?

Use a **Schema Registry** (available in Event Hubs) or adopt versioned schema files stored in source control.

Best practices:

- Use **Avro** or **JSON Schema** to define contracts

- Version schemas explicitly (eventType: OrderCreated.v2)
- Validate messages before publishing
- Use CI to ensure backward compatibility

Can I use Logic Apps with Service Bus or Event Grid?

Yes. Logic Apps has native connectors for all messaging services.

Example:

- **Trigger**: New message in Service Bus queue
- **Action**: Call HTTP API, update database, or post to Teams
- **Output**: Publish to Event Grid custom topic

Use Logic Apps for integration-heavy, low-code workflows.

How do I configure private access?

Use **Private Endpoints** and disable public network access.

Steps:

1. Create Private Endpoint in same VNet
2. Approve connection from Service Bus/Event Grid/Event Hub
3. Update DNS to point to private IP

Ensure RBAC and NSG rules are configured correctly.

How long are events retained?

- **Service Bus**:
  - Queue retention up to 14 days
- **Event Hubs**:
  - Retention up to 90 days (Basic/Premium)
- **Event Grid**:
  - Transient delivery only (24-hour retry window)

For long-term replay, use **Event Hubs Capture** or persist to **Data Lake.**

Summary

These frequently asked questions address common points of friction, design confusion, and operational hurdles in Azure's messaging landscape. Whether planning, deploying, scaling, or troubleshooting, returning to these answers helps reduce complexity and aligns your implementation with best practices. As Azure evolves, continuously review documentation and changelogs to stay aligned with new capabilities and guidance.

www.ingramcontent.com/pod-product-compliance
Lightning Source LLC
LaVergne TN
LVHW090258210926
848480LV00001B/68